MODERN AUSTRALIAN POETRY

H. M. GREEN

MODERN AUSTRALIAN POETRY

Selected by

H. M. GREEN

Second Edition Revised

Granger Poetry Library

GRANGER BOOK CO., INC.
Great Neck, NY

First Published 1946
Second Edition, revised, 1952
Reprinted 1979

INTERNATIONAL STANDARD BOOK NUMBER
0-89609-113-9

LIBRARY OF CONGRESS CATALOG NUMBER
78-73487

PRINTED IN THE UNITED STATES OF AMERICA

INTRODUCTORY TO THE SECOND EDITION

THE second edition of this anthology is, it is hoped, a better and a more representative collection than the first. About a dozen poems have been omitted, mostly because they did not stand comparison with the company in which they were placed, and a couple of dozen have been added. But almost all the additional poems are by authors who were already represented in the first edition, but who have gone on producing good work. There are also several poems belonging to the Angry Penguin group, which were not available before. But even including these, only four new authors are represented, and not all of them are young and at the beginning of their development; new poets of marked ability have been comparatively rare lately. And several of our leading poets seem now to have attained or almost attained their full powers. It may be that the remarkable uprush of poetry in this country during the last decade is beginning to slacken, though allowance must be made for the rising cost of publishing, which makes things harder for the newcomer.

The plan and organization of the anthology remain the same. The postponing of the signatures to the end of the book, not altogether a novelty as a matter of fact, seems now to have been accepted, though it is said that one invincible conservative took the trouble to look up and add the signatures in what he considered to be their primordially determined places, at the end of the poems! And the arrangement into categories, all but the first of which are supposed to merge in one another, also remains. So we still begin with a series intended to illustrate Australia and her development, and continue with 'intellectual' poems, mystic and symbolic poems, poems of history, legend and fantasy, poems of beauty and love, of death and hate and war; though here and there the order has been altered or one poem substituted for another with the object of making the scheme clearer.

The introduction to the first edition is repeated as it stood, except for a correction of fact and one slight omission. There seems no reason to qualify any of its general statements, and the truth of one of them has been reinforced. To the leading Australian poets may now be added Judith Wright and James McAuley, though McAuley has published comparatively little

v

as yet; and, with FitzGerald and Slessor, Wright now takes her place among the principal poets writing in English today. Since the achievement of these four is not yet universally recognized in their own country, it is scarcely surprising that it is quite unrecognized overseas. The inclusion of some of their poems, as well as of poems by such older writers as Brennan, Neilson, McCrae and Mary Gilmore, would strengthen English anthologies. It would also help to modify the impression of sameness that attaches to modern English poetry, for whereas English poets fall naturally into groups, in Australia the follow-my-leader tendency is comparatively slight, and most poets create their own little worlds.

Australian literature has always been strongest in poetry, and during the last ten years or so Australian poetry has made a place for itself in the literary world which can be disregarded only by those who are not acquainted with it.

INTRODUCTORY TO THE FIRST EDITION

THE material from which this anthology has been drawn over-
laps one of those rather indefinite boundaries that separate
natural periods; the period of romantic nationalism and the
period of modernity and disillusion, which faded into one an-
other soon after the end of the first world war. But for several
reasons the differences between the work of the older and the
younger poets in the anthology are, as will be seen, not such as
to divide it into two parts. The older poets represent the more
reflective aspect of the romantic era, which in the literature of
Australia is not so far removed from the intellectualism of the
moderns, except for a section of extremist poets which is neither
large nor influential. So, for example, Brennan and FitzGerald
fit well together in spite of the generation that lies between
them; though it is true they fit all the better because they have
something in common and because FitzGerald has been in-
fluenced by Brennan. And in the work of one or two of the
older poets, McCrae for example, there is an element of time-
lessness; McCrae belongs to several other ages besides, indeed
even more than, the two he happens to have lived in. There
are other 'timeless' poems—some of McCuaig's for example—
in the younger part of the collection also, which help to bridge
the gap between the two generations. Besides, the gap is not
nearly so wide here as in Britain. By reason of the time-lag that
is always observable in the literature of a young and far-off
country, 'modernism' is even now a comparatively new thing in
Australia. The first wave of modernism in verse—the wave
represented by T. S. Eliot—did not reach these shores in any
unmistakable form until the publication of Slessor's *Cuckooz
Contrey*, as late as 1932. Of our other 'moderns', the most
noteworthy, FitzGerald, Hope and McAuley for example, avoid
extremism and show no traces of the influence of any individual
poet of the present day; and among the general run of poets in
this country there seems to be less inclination towards intellec-
tualist and formal (or perhaps one should say informal) extremes
than among English poets. So that on the whole, though the
contents of this little book are varied enough—romance and real-
ism, regular and irregular rhythms, aspiration and disillusion-

ment, dryness and sweetness all mingled—yet they do, I think, blend into something like the voice of Australian poetry today.

The voice, or should I say the voices? For though if one glances over these poems at haphazard they seem exceedingly diverse, yet internal differences gradually diminish in the perception of a common bond. The diversity exists within a homogeneity; if it is not a voice one hears, but voices, they combine and blend into a chorale, in which one may imagine Brennan as a bass, Neilson as a tenor, and McCrae as a rich baritone. And what differentiates this chorale from others is that the singers are Australians. Their poems, or the most representative of them, share, though to a smaller extent, the realism, sophistication, detachment, disillusion—and, as to method, the tendency to psychological analysis and disdain of convention—that mark the generality of today's younger poets all over the world. But they share something else also. Although the nationalism that inspired the Australian writers of the 'nineties and early nineteen-hundreds is now out of date, among some of our writers another nationalism is growing up. It has two main centres, *Meanjin Papers*, formerly of Brisbane, now of Melbourne, and the Jindyworobak Club of Adelaide, which have provided an inspiration, a war-cry and a rallying ground for many of our younger poets, and for some of our older poets as well. During the making of this anthology *Meanjin* has developed from a leaflet containing verse only to one of our two leading literary magazines, and it is represented here by a number of poems. But though *Meanjin* is a centre, there is no such thing as a Meanjin movement; the magazine is open to all kinds of verse, and to British and American as well as to Australian writers. Jindyworobakism on the other hand is a movement, though of late its doctrine has widened and at the same time the movement has lost force. Its principal example here is a clear-cut little cameo of Mudie's, which expresses the Jindyworobak doctrine in an extreme form, though it is included simply on its merits as a poem. But with hardly an exception the Australian quality of these poems is implicit though it is widespread. It will be most evident, no doubt, in the introductory group of poems, whose subjects are all Australian, but is by no means confined to this group. Among our better known poets, qualities that may be regarded as definitely Australian are

evident in Kenneth Slessor for example, who contrives to com-
bine in a style that is highly individual, something of the dry-
ness and disillusion of the early Eliot with a cynical flavour that
is his own and that is Australian also, together with an enthu-
siasm that he, like some other Australians, feels but tries to sup-
press. In several of Slessor's poems, notably *Country Towns*, a
traditional and universal theme is treated in a manner that is
modern and Australian at the same time. And though Fitz-
Gerald's work contains little local colour, his fresh and confident
energy separates him by a world's width from the overseas
intellectuals with whom in other respects he might be grouped.
Even McCrae, at first glance English, and traditionally English,
to the core, is Australian in the freshness and warmth and
tropical exuberance of his feeling and colouring, and in his easy
unconstraint and disregard for conventional dominances, not
all of which can be illustrated in this anthology. And even in
Brennan, least 'Australian' of our poets, may be found many
traces of an Australian environment and upbringing; see for
example, of his poems reprinted, *Fire in the heavens*, whose
subject is in an old Australian tradition, founded by Harpur in
his *Midsummer Noon in the Australian Forest*. Other examples
of Australianism in these poems are not hard to find. In Mary
Gilmore, for instance: most of her themes are universal, but can
one imagine her work, as a whole, emanating from any other
country than this? And it seems to me that certain mental and
emotional attributes which may be accepted as Australian, not of
course because they do not exist elsewhere, but because they are
more representative here, are apparent throughout. They may
be found, I think, in the work of poets so different as Leonard
Mann, Ronald McCuaig and A. D. Hope for example.

The diversity of the contents of the anthology is too obvious
to need illustration; seeing that Australians are generally ad-
mitted to be unusually individualized, this should not come as a
surprise. Indeed I doubt whether the far greater volume of
English or American poetry today covers a wider range. As to
standard it is another matter, but at least one can say that now
for the first time in the short history of Australian literature
there is a basis for comparison with the work of poets overseas.
A local critic has declared that 'Australian poetry of the last

century (that is, since 1900) can hold its own, in its highest expression, with any poetry written during the same period in the English tongue.' If that were true it would mean that the best of Brennan, Baylebridge, McCrae, Neilson, FitzGerald, Slessor, let us say, could hold its own with the best of Yeats, Eliot, Pound, Housman, Auden, Spender and so on. I shouldn't like to swear to that. But if we narrowed the comparison to poets alive and at their best today, and then narrowed it again to a comparison involving only a few of the most noteworthy on either side, we should be much nearer the mark. Leaving out American poetry for the sake of convenience, how would Fitz-Gerald and Slessor compare with Auden and Spender, for example? The two Australian poets have produced far less, but FitzGerald's *Essay on Memory* and Slessor's *Five Bells* seem to me comparable with Auden's and Spender's best poems. On the other hand, after the two leaders in Australia there are fewer runners-up, and the rank and file are infinitely fewer in Australia; but this is leading us rather beyond our present scope.

The general scheme of the arrangement of the poems should be fairly evident; it need only be said that an attempt has been made to combine natural fitness of association with an occasional element of surprise. Some readers may find it interesting to sort out the 'natural groups' and see how they fade into one another, or to find reasons for or against the inclusion of a particular poem, or for giving or not giving it the position it here occupies. The signatures have been omitted because the aim of the anthology is to give an impression of modern Australian poetry as a whole and in its various aspects, rather than to illustrate the work of individual poets. But if the reader wants to know who wrote a particular poem, he has only to turn to the Title and Author Index at the end of the book; or if he wants to know whether a particular poet is represented, and by what poems, there is an Author and Title Index.

Something about the title, which is to say the subject, of the anthology.

Of modernity, the test used has been tone rather than time. None of these poems was published much more than about a generation ago; but some have been left out that would have to be included in any purely historical anthology. This has, in at least one case, involved some sacrifice. Although Bernard O'Dowd holds a high place in Australian poetry, permission has not been asked to use any of his work, because in more ways than one it 'dates'. The anthology has, in fact, been deliberately confined to poems whose outlook and method ought not to seem strange to a present-day reader whose taste is fairly catholic. The idea has been to afford a general impression of the uppermost layer of Australian poetry; of Australian poetry as it is, broadly speaking, today.

By Australian poetry is meant poetry written by Australians; that is, by poets domiciled here; or who, if they have gone to live abroad, have at least become Australians again for the time. New Zealand poets have not been included; the Australian and New Zealand literatures are at different stages and are developing along different lines, and each country is producing enough poetry nowadays for an anthology of its own.

The term 'poetry' here excludes the ballad. The aim of the balladist is, as a rule, quite distinct from that of the poet. Whereas the poet's aim is to convey something, in which ideally there is no distinction between form and substance, the typical balladist sets out to tell a story, or perhaps to describe something, using verse merely, or at least mainly, as a medium. Therefore, though Australia has produced a number of fine ballads, of which many are poetic in places and a few are poems, it has seemed best not to mingle the two kinds of verse, particularly in a small anthology.

This anthology draws, then, only upon Australian writers, only upon poets as distinct from balladists, and only upon those poets who may reasonably be considered modern. It will be obvious not merely that its standard is variable and its contents uneven, but that some of its omissions are better than some of its inclusions. The aim has been to represent modern Australian poetry at its best, it is true, but also in its variety; if all the best had been included and all the rest rejected there would not have been half so many authors or anything like the range of subject and treatment. In accordance with this aim, one or two of the longer poems are represented here by extracts, though occasionally even a short poem has (by permission) been reduced where it is repetitive, or where its quality is markedly unequal. One of the longer poems, FitzGerald's *Essay on Memory*, is given in full. The author did not feel able to consent to its being cut, and without FitzGerald at his best the collection would have been incomplete and far less representative. I regret not being allowed to include anything by William Baylebridge. A few well-known poems have been omitted on the ground that they have been published in anthology after anthology until they are shop-worn; but it has, I think, been possible to substitute in each case another less known poem by the same author without serious sacrifice. An attempt has been made to select the best, not necessarily the most characteristic, of a writer's work; for example, the selection from Hopegood may surprise some readers. Next, poems that refuse to reveal even what they are talking about, except after an amount of study disproportionate to the difficulty of the thought involved, have been excluded deliberately. Nevertheless I should have liked to include a couple of partial exceptions by members of our principal extremist group, the Angry Penguins.

Such a collection as this should afford an indication for the future. Only a few years ago it was possible to write that the prospects of Australian poetry were not bright, since almost all of our young writers were turning to the novel. Such a statement today would be quite wrong. FitzGerald and Slessor are young yet and still developing, and McAuley, Hope, H. F. Stewart, Kenneth Mackenzie and several other less known poets might conceivably any day produce something quite out of the common.

The typescript for this anthology was handed in as long ago as February 1945. Nothing published since then has been included, unless it had been already selected from manuscript. The single exception is McAuley's *Sirius*, which was too good to miss.

MODERN
AUSTRALIAN
POETRY

VESPERS

BEAUTY is gone from the hills, the high brooks are forsaken;
the thorn rock-rooted, the sunny covert, the long upland
    shoulders
are empty; the hawk, low-wheeling, from his windy station
descries no lands unknown, no voice in the air discovers.

Yet the hill stands and shoulders in air his unshaken summit;
cleaves the thorn to the stone; while low in the eddying heaven
the hawk hangs dreamless, awaiting a dark wind's coming,
the unchanging shade, the high stars ascending.

UNDERGROUND

Deep flows the flood,
deep under the land.
Dark is it, and blood
and eucalypt color and scent it.
Deep flows the stream,
feeding the totem-roots,
deep through the time of dream
in Alcheringa.
Deep flows the river,
deep as our roots reach for it;
feeding us, angry and striving
against the blindness
ship-fed seas bring us
from colder waters.

SHIP FROM THAMES

STAY, ship from Thames, with fettered sails
in Sydney Cove this ebb of tide;
your gear untangled from the gales,
imprisoned at your anchor ride.

The portly gentlemen, who are
the pillars of the land, come down
and greet the Newcomes voyaged far
to make a name in Sydney Town.

The redcoats, too, with shouldered arms,
marshal pale wretches from the hold,
who, cramped in tempests and in calms,
have learned to do as they are told.

Flash phaetons fill the streets to-day;
inn-tables rock to sailor fists;
the Governor, while the town is gay,
checks over new assignment lists.

Aloof, the slandered and abhorred
behold from off a quarried rise
the cause of all the stir abroad,
a fiercer glitter in their eyes.

FIRE IN THE HEAVENS

FIRE in the heavens, and fire along the hills,
and fire made solid in the flinty stone,
thick-mass'd or scatter'd pebble, fire that fills
the breathless hour that lives in fire alone.

This valley, long ago the patient bed
of floods that carv'd its antient amplitude,
in stillness of the Egyptian crypt outspread,
endures to drown in noon-day's tyrant mood.

Behind the veil of burning silence bound,
vast life's innumerous busy littleness
is hush'd in vague-conjectured blur of sound
that dulls the brain with slumbrous weight, unless

some dazzling puncture let the stridence throng
in the cicada's torture-point of song.

IN THE DAY'S WORK

WE left the homestead at break of day,
And into the desert we rode away.
There was arid rock on either hand,
Veiled with drifting, red-brown sand,
And nothing the aching silence stirred,
No insect's chirr nor song of bird,
Just desolate, silent loneliness:
The creak of leather, the ashy hiss
Of loose sand falling to Gunnar's tread
Were all that moved, in that land of dread.
All river-beds were parched and dry,
Their hot rocks bare to the blazing sky;
And I'd dream at night of waterfalls,
Dashing down their rocky walls;
Of rivers flowing, deep and cool,
And many a placid woodland pool,
Where lilies bloomed at the water's brink,
And shy bush-creatures stooped to drink.
Then I'd wake, to heat, and sand, and thirst
In that desolate land that God had cursed.
On the desert's rim one pool we found,
Choked with beasts that had long lain drowned.
My nigger dropped from his horse with a shout,
Raked rotting hides and bones all out,
Gulping the fetid ooze of the soak,
While I sat and cursed, in a strangled croak.
My throat was parched, as dry as hell,
But I dared not drink from that reeking well.
So we turned our faces south again,
Where heatwaves danced on the arid plain,
On the hard brown earth, 'neath a brazen sky,
Where wings of Death went drifting by.

BULLOCKY

Beside his heavy-shouldered team,
thirsty with drought and chilled with rain,
he weathered all the striding years
till they ran widdershins in his brain:

Till the long solitary tracks
etched deeper with each lurching load
were populous before his eyes,
and fiends and angels used his road.

·All the long straining journey grew
a mad apocalyptic dream,
and he old Moses, and the slaves
his suffering and stubborn team.

Then in his evening camp beneath
the half-light pillars of the trees
he filled the steepled cone of night
with shouted prayers and prophecies.

While past the camp fire's crimson ring
the star-struck darkness cupped him round,
and centuries of cattlebells
rang with their sweet uneasy sound.

Grass is across the waggon-tracks,
and plough strikes bone beneath the grass,
and vineyards cover all the slopes
where the dead teams were used to pass.

O vine, grow close upon that bone
and hold it with your rooted hand.
The prophet Moses feeds the grape,
and fruitful is the Promised Land.

A PIONEER OF MONARO

I HAVE loved two things deeply: the earth and silence,
Two giant bulks furrowed by cold harmony,
Petrified rhythms, with eternal rhythmic challenge.
Peace bound me to this land—peace in three shapes:
The colour, the shadow, the noiseless mountains beyond.
Here, between the beach and the mystic Centre
I shape a forming foothold and the future;
If I have grown quiet as my land, remember
That to conquer mountains one must think as a mountain.
And these still places wherein, with no flutter or tumult
My being will gutter and dissolve, owe me one debt:
That I, foe of time, be not utterly extinguished;
Who robs me of this due has my only hatred.

I know this Boyd: a builder of lighthouse-towers
Maintained for his own craft only—let others perish;
That squared stone is his own monument.
He has given us other samples of his building:
An evil town, veined with corruption and murder,
Clinging like a swollen leech to the bay's lips.

He does not love this country—why come here
Trampling my peace, trampling my very life?
He holds all the cards—even time is with him,
Time, lover of anything gaudy, hollow, rotten.

If he and I were dead I might grapple his ghost;
No money or influence could help him then,
And yet I should go down—he is the stronger.

Time and a legend stealing my name from the earth.

THE STOCKMAN

THE sun was in the summer grass,
  The coolibahs were twisted steel:
The stockman paused beneath their shade
  And sat upon his heel,
And with the reins looped through his arm
He rolled tobacco in his palm.

His horse stood still. His cattle dog
  Tongued in the shadow of the tree,
And for a moment on the plain
  Time waited for the three.
And then the stockman licked his fag
And Time took up his solar swag.

I saw the stockman mount and ride
  Across the mirage on the plain;
And still that timeless moment brought
  Fresh ripples to my brain:
It seemed in that distorting air
I saw his grandson sitting there.

CLEARING FOR THE PLOUGH

THROUGH tranquil years they watched the changes
Creep over hill and plain; they saw
The kangaroo go from his ranges,
The clucking emu come no more.

And then the Blacks, with startled faces
Broke off the dance where laughter sprang
Naked and free; and the old places
Forgot the spear and boomerang.

And over plain and hill there drifted
Sheep numberless and meek and brown
That grazed all day in peace and lifted
Low bleatings when the sun went down.

But the great gums watched on, unknowing
What time was saying, could they hear:
'The end has come of bloom and growing,
The blade and the red fire are near.

The round of change is sure and steady:
The kangaroo, the sheep, the plough.
The axe is ground and bright and ready,
The sleeve is rolled—and it's your turn now!'

. . . . . .

The stars, when the long nights close over,
Will miss them in the accustomed spot,
And the great sun who was their lover
Will come each day and find them not.

And winds that laughed to see them shaken
To mighty song, will pause and pass
Half loath, for sorrow, to awaken
The lesser music of the grass.

THE SELECTOR'S WIFE

THE quick compunction cannot serve;
She saw the flash,
Ere he had bent with busy hand
And drooping lash.

She saw him mark for the first time,
With critic eye,
What five years' heavy toil had done
'Neath roof and sky.

And always now so sensitive
Her poor heart is,
That moment will push in between
His kindest kiss.

The moment when he realised
Her girlhood done—
The truth her glass had long revealed
Of beauty gone.

Until some future gracious flash
Shall let each know
That that which drew and holds him yet
Shall never go.

PASTORAL

THE farmer turns for home; his team's glad tread
    Drums from the furrows red,
    Passing where bronze sheep graze
        In brass-bright haze.

In kitchen wide, the grooved gold pumpkins' sheen
    And apples' palest green
    Are small gay suns, whose light
        Mocks high roof's night.

Beside the bustling fire two young lambs bleat,
    Then run on clacking feet,
    Kneel, and in bowls of milk
        Dip mouths of silk.

In hail-green sky, glass-clear as silver rain,
    Above cool hills and plain
    And fallows dark as plums,
        The first star comes.

Tendrils of mist entwine the moonlit wheat.
    Noises of small wild feet
    Scurry through high bleached grass.
        Swans call and pass.

Night's purple vine is trellised on the sky,
    Bright grapes are hung on high;
    Mirroring waters hold
        Rare fruits of gold.

A cold south wind drifts by the sleeping farms.
    His young wife lifts round arms,
    Binds him within a snare
        Of gleaming hair.

They laugh and love within the shadowed room.
    Afar, War snarls his doom—
    'Slay and be slain. Hard years
        Will dry her tears.'

WINTER WESTERLIES

LEANING against the wind across the paddock ways
Comes Dan home with forward stoop like a man bent and old,
Clashes the door in haste as one pursued: 'By Christ it's cold!'
And crooks his fingers to the blaze.

We do not live these days, but each exhausting day
Unnerved we numbly wait return of life, and must abide
The wind, the still beleaguering wind; all voices else outside
Imperiously it has blown away.

Over the bronze-brown paddocks the grass is bowed flat down;
Along the birdless creek a cold malevolence has passed;
A forlorn sparrow clings on the fence against the icy blast,
His soft breast feathers loosely blown.

We watch the saplings buffeted without repose,
Their foliage all on one side, plunging without rest,
Stems leaning all one way from the assailing west,
Bending as backs cower from blows.

The hunched cattle no longer feeding dejected stand
With dumb endurance, tails to the flogging wind hour after
    hour;
From some far frozen hell of winds a blind and soulless power
Invades and harries all the land.

The wind! The wind! It fumbles at the fastened panes,
Fills and possesses all, a tyranny without control;
Ceaseless, changeless, malign, searching into the very soul
The rushing desolation reigns.

COUNTRY TOWNS

COUNTRY towns, with your willows and squares,
And farmers bouncing on barrel mares
To public-houses of yellow wood
With '1860' over their doors,
And that mysterious race of Hogans
Which always keeps General Stores. . . .

At the School of Arts, a broadsheet lies
Sprayed with the sarcasm of flies:
'The Great Golightly Family
Of Entertainers Here To-night'—
Dated a year and a half ago,
But left there, less from carelessness
Than from a wish to seem polite.

Verandas baked with musky sleep,
Mulberry faces dozing deep,
And dogs that lick the sunlight up
Like paste of gold—or, roused in vain
By far, mysterious buggy-wheels,
Lower their ears, and drowse again. . . .

Country towns with your schooner bees,
And locusts burnt in the pepper-trees,
Drown me with syrups, arch your boughs,
Find me a bench, and let me snore,
Till, charged with ale and unconcern,
I'll think it's noon at half-past four!

From LAST TRAMS

THEN, from the skeletons of trams,
Gazing at lighted rooms, you'll find
The black and Röntgen diagrams
Of window-plants across the blind

That print their knuckleduster sticks,
Their buds of gum, against the light
Like negatives of candlesticks
Whose wicks are lit by fluorite;

And shapes look out, or bodies pass,
Between the darkness and the flare,
Between the curtain and the glass,
Of men and women moving there.

So through the moment's needle-eye,
Like phantoms in the window-chink,
Their faces brush you as they fly,
Fixed in the shutters of a blink;

But whose they are, intent on what,
Who knows? They rattle into void,
Stars of a film without a plot,
Snippings of idiot celluloid.

NO, NOT THE OWL

No, not the owl, the kookaburra
  Is wisdom's Delphic bird,
Divining how creation's circuits
  Arrive at the absurd.

The mumpish owl naively mumbles
  His monody of night;
Unawed, the jackass greets with chuckles
  Pomp of day's western flight.

So, when death strives to be impressive
  As battle's ghostly guest,
Undaunted diggers, just as drily,
  Crack a sardonic jest.

THE BUNYIP

THE water down the rocky wall
Lets fall its shining stair;
The bunyip in the deep green pool
Looks up it to the air.

The kookaburra drank, he says, then shrieked at me with
    laughter,
I dragged him down in a hairy hand and ate his thighbones after;
My head is bruised with the falling foam, the water blinds my
    eye,
Yet I will climb that waterfall and walk upon the sky.

The turpentine and stringybark,
The dark red bloodwoods lean
And drop their shadows in the pool
With blue sky in between.

A beast am I, the bunyip says, my voice a drowning cow's,
Yet am I not a singing bird among these waving boughs?
I raise my black and dripping head, I cry a bubbling cry,
For I shall climb the trunks of trees to walk upon the sky.

Gold and red the gum-trees glow,
Yellow gleam the ferns;
The bunyip in the crimson pool
Believes the water burns.

I know the roots of rocks, he says, I know the door of hell;
I ate the abo's daughter once, I know my faults full well;
Yet sunset walks between the trees and sucks the water dry,
And when the whole world's burnt away I'll walk upon the sky.

The little frogs they call like bells,
The bunyip swims alone;
Across the pool the stars are laid
Like stone by silver stone.

What did I do before I was born, the bunyip asks the night;
I looked at myself in the water's glass and I nearly died of fright;
Condemned to haunt a pool in the bush while a thousand years
    go by—
Yet I walk on the stars like stepping-stones and I'll climb them
    into the sky.

A lady walks across the night
And sees that mirror there;
Oh, is it for herself alone
The moon lets down her hair?

The yabbie's back is green for her, his claws are opal-blue,
Look for my soul, the bunyip says, for it was a jewel too.
I bellowed with woe to the yabbie once, but all I said was a lie,
For I'll catch the moon by her silver hair and dance her around
    the sky.

AUSTRALIA

A NATION of trees, drab green and desolate grey
In the field uniform of modern wars
Darkens her hills those endless, outstretched paws
Of Sphinx demolished or stone lion worn away.

They call her a young country, but they lie:
She is the last of lands, the emptiest,
A woman beyond her change of life, a breast
Still tender but within the womb is dry;

Without songs, architecture, history:
The emotions and superstitions of younger lands.
Her rivers of water drown among inland sands,
The river of her immense stupidity

Floods her monotonous tribes from Cairns to Perth.
In them at last the ultimate men arrive
Whose boast is not: 'we live' but 'we survive'
A type who will inhabit the dying earth.

And her five cities, like five teeming sores
Each drains her: a vast parasite robber-state
Where second-hand Europeans pullulate
Timidly on the edge of alien shores.

Yet there are some like me turn gladly home
From the lush jungle of modern thought, to find
The Arabian desert of the human mind,
Hoping, if still from the deserts the prophets come,

Such savage and scarlet as no green hills dare
Springs in that waste, some spirit which escapes
The learned doubt, the chatter of cultured apes
Which is called civilization over there.

C

From THE WANDERER

WHEN window-lamps had dwindled, then I rose
and left the town behind me; and on my way
passing a certain door I stopt, remembering
how once I stood on its threshold, and my life
was offer'd to me, a road how different
from that of the years since gone! and I had but
to rejoin an olden path, once dear, since left.
All night I have walk'd and my heart was deep awake,
remembering ways I dream'd and that I chose,
remembering lucidly, and was not sad,
being brimm'd with all the liquid and clear dark
of the night that was not stirr'd with any tide;
for leaves were silent and the road gleam'd pale,
following the ridge, and I was alone with night.
But now I am come among the rougher hills
and grow aware of the sea that somewhere near
is restless; and the flood of night is thinn'd
and stars are whitening. O, what horrible dawn
will bare me the way and crude lumps of the hills
and the homeless concave of the day, and bare
the ever-restless, ever-complaining sea?

Each day I see the long ships coming into port
and the people crowding to their rail, glad of the shore:
because to have been alone with the sea and not to have known
of anything happening in any crowded way,
and to have heard no other voice than the crooning sea's
has charmed away the old rancours, and the great winds
have search'd and swept their hearts of the old irksome thoughts:
so, to their freshen'd gaze, each land smiles a good home.
Why envy I, seeing them made gay to greet the shore?
Surely I do not foolishly desire to go
hither and thither upon the earth and grow weary
with seeing many lands and peoples and the sea:
but if I might, some day, landing I reck not where
have heart to find a welcome and perchance a rest,
I would spread the sail to any wandering wind of the air
this night, when waves are hard and rain blots out the land.

I am driven everywhere from a clinging home,
O autumn eves! and I ween'd that you would yet
have made, when your smouldering dwindled to odorous fume,
close room for my heart, where I might crouch and dream
of days and ways I had trod, and look with regret
on the darkening homes of men and the window-gleam,
and forget the morrows that threat and the unknown way.
But a bitter wind came out of the yellow-pale west
and my heart is shaken and fill'd with its triumphing cry:
You shall find neither home nor rest; for ever you roam
with stars as they drift and wilful fates of the sky!

. . . . . .

Once I could sit by the fire hourlong when the dripping eaves
sang cheer to the shelter'd, and listen, and know that the woods
    drank full,
and think of the morn that was coming and how the freshen'd
    leaves
would glint in the sun and the dusk beneath would be bright
    and cool.

Now, when I hear, I am cold within: for my mind drifts wide
where the blessing is shed for naught on the salt waste of the sea,
on the valleys that hold no rest and the hills that may not abide:
and the fire loses its warmth and my home is far from me.

How old is my heart, how old, how old is my heart,
and did I ever go forth with song when the morn was new?
I seem to have trod on many ways: I seem to have left
I know not how many homes; and to leave each
was still to leave a portion of mine own heart,
of my old heart whose life I had spent to make that home
and all I had was regret, and a memory.

So I sit and muse in this wayside harbour and wait
till I hear the gathering cry of the ancient winds and again
I must up and out and leave the embers of the hearth
to crumble silently into white ash and dust,
and see the road stretch bare and pale before me: again
my garment and my home shall be the enveloping winds
and my heart be fill'd wholly with their old pitiless cry.

. . . . . .

You, at whose table I have sat, some distant eve
beside the road, and eaten and you pitied me
to be driven an aimless way before the pitiless winds,
how much ye have given and knew not, pitying foolishly!
For not alone the bread I broke, but I tasted too
all your unwitting lives and knew the narrow soul
that bodies it in the landmarks of your fields,
and broods dumbly within your little seasons' round,
where, after sowing, comes the short-lived summer's mirth,
and, after harvesting, the winter's lingering dream,
half memory and regret, half hope, crouching beside
the hearth that is your only centre of life and dream.
And knowing the world how limitless and the way how long,
and the home of man how feeble and builded on the winds,
I have lived your life, that eve, as you might never live
knowing, and pity you, if you should come to know.

I cry to you as I pass your windows in the dusk:

Ye have built you unmysterious homes and ways in the wood
where of old ye went with sudden eyes to the right and left;
and your going was now made safe and your staying comforted,
for the forest edge itself, holding old savagery
in unsearch'd glooms, was your houses' friendly barrier.
And now that the year goes winterward, ye thought to hide
behind your gleaming panes, and where the hearth sings merrily
make cheer with meat and wine, and sleep in the long night,
and the uncared wastes might be a crying unhappiness.
But I, who have come from the outer night, I say to you
the winds are up and terribly will they shake the dry wood:
the woods shall awake, hearing them, shall awake to be toss'd
      and riven,
and make a cry and a parting in your sleep all night
as the wither'd leaves go whirling all night along all ways.
And when ye come forth at dawn, uncomforted by sleep,
ye shall stand at amaze, beholding all the ways overhidden
with worthless drift of the dead and all your broken world:
and ye shall not know whence the winds have come, nor shall
      ye know
whither the yesterdays have fled, or if they were.

Come out, come out, ye souls that serve, why will ye die?
or will ye sit and stifle in your prison-homes
dreaming of some master that holds the winds in leash
and the waves of darkness yonder in the gaunt hollow of night?
nay, there is none that rules: all is a strife of the winds
and the night shall billow in storm full oft ere all be done.
For this is the hard doom that is laid on all of you,
to be that whereof ye dream, dreaming against your will.
But first ye must travel the many ways, and your close-wrapt
    souls
must be blown thro' with the rain that comes from the homeless
    dark:
for until ye have had care of the wastes there shall be no truce
for them nor you, nor home, but ever the ancient feud;
and the soul of man must house the cry of the darkling waves
as he follows the ridge above the waters shuddering towards
    night,
and the rains and the winds that roam anhunger'd for some
    heart's warmth.
Go: tho' ye find it bitter, yet must ye be bare
to the wind and the sea and the night and the wail of birds in
    the sky;
go: tho' the going be hard and the goal blinded with rain
yet the staying is a death that is never soften'd with sleep.

Dawns of the world, how I have known you all,
so many, and so varied, and the same!
dawns o'er the timid plains, or in the folds
of the arm'd hills, or by the unsleeping shore;
a chill touch on the chill flesh of the dark
that, shuddering, shrinks from its couch, and leaves
a homeless light, staring, disconsolate,
on the drear world it knows too well, the world
it fled and finds again, its wistful hope
unmet by any miracle of night,
that mocks it rather, with its shreds that hang
about the woods and huddled bulks of gloom
that crouch, malicious, in the broken combes,
witness to foulnesses else unreveal'd
that visit earth and violate her dreams
in the lone hours when only evil wakes.

What is there with you and me, that I may not forget
but your white shapes come crowding noiselessly in my nights,
making my sleep a flight from a thousand beckoning hands?
Was it not enough that your cry dwelt in my waking ears
that now, seeking oblivion, I must yet be haunted
by each black maw of hunger that yawns despairingly
a moment ere its whitening frenzy bury it?
O waves of all the seas, would I could give you peace
and find my peace again: for all my peace is fled
and broken and blown along your white delirious crests!

O desolate eves along the way, how oft,
despite your bitterness, was I warm at heart!
not with the glow of remember'd hearths, but warm
with the solitary unquenchable fire that burns
a flameless heat deep in his heart who has come
where the formless winds plunge and exult for aye
among the naked spaces of the world,
far past the circle of the ruddy hearths
and all their memories. Desperate eves,
when the wind-bitten hills turn'd violet
along their rims, and the earth huddled her heat
within her niggard bosom, and the dead stones
lay battle-strewn before the iron wind
that, blowing from the chill west, made all its way
a loneliness to yield its triumph room;
yet in that wind a clamour of trumpets rang,
old trumpets, resolute, stark, undauntable,
singing to battle against the eternal foe,
the wronger of this world, and all his powers
in some last fight, foredoom'd disastrous,
upon the final ridges of the world:
a war-worn note, stern fire in the stricken eve,
and fire thro' all my ancient heart, that sprang
towards that last hope of a glory won in defeat,
whence, knowing not sure if such high grace befall
at the end, yet I draw courage to front the way.

The land I came thro' last was dumb with night,
a limbo of defeated glory, a ghost:
for wreck of constellations flicker'd perishing

27

scarce sustain'd in the mortuary air,
and on the ground and out of livid pools
wreck of old swords and crowns glimmer'd at whiles;
I seem'd at home in some old dream of kingship: •
now it is clear grey day and the road is plain,
I am the wanderer of many years
who cannot tell if ever he was king
or if ever kingdoms were: I know I am
the wanderer of the ways of all the worlds,
to whom the sunshine and the rain are one
and one to stay or hasten, because he knows
no ending of the way, no home, no goal,
and phantom night and the grey day alike
withhold the heart where all my dreams and days
might faint in soft fire and delicious death:
and saying this to myself as a simple thing
I feel a peace fall in the heart of the winds
and a clear dusk settle, somewhere, far in me.

ESSAY ON MEMORY

RAIN in my ears: impatiently there raps
at a sealed door the fury of chill drops—
knuckles bared of the flesh come rattling on
vaults that conceal a sorrier skeleton
huddled, unhearing, in a dark so deep
that this clear summons ruffles not calm sleep.

It is the hand of Memory come scratching
on the tomb of carrion buried from mankind—
forgotten by all except this body-snatching
walker of old night and times dropped from mind,
who knows where the slain rots and seeks it yet;
for Memory does not fail though men forget,
but pokes a ghost-finger into all our pies
and jabs out the dead meat, a grim Jack Horner,
mocking the mild dream, half guess, half lies,
of History babbling from his chimney-corner.

Memory is not that picture tacked on thought
among the show-girls and prize-ribbon rams,
wherein is last week's yesterday to be sought,
lens-twisted and fading, and yet somehow caught
in the known gesture, almost at speaking terms;
nor is it the sky-old story which in stone
within baked saurian footmarks prints its own,
as if the mud might soften and recollect
almost our lean beginnings and project
against the background of these days some far
horrible firmament, or show a star
choking with cloud whereunder, oozed from slime,
slow forms are dragging—half-way back through time;
nor is it composite mind whose cells are men
and whose dour genius grafts great stone on stone
by torch-flare lit on torch-flare—till it seems
that the tall topwork of new cornice gleams
in the glow of ancient lore, and sits firm-stayed
in masonry that hands long cold once laid.

Something of all this . . . but Memory peers
from the brown mottled ruin, shrieks and gibbers

among the fallen fragments of lost years,
lurks by the lichened archway, frights the neighbours
when a wind shrills about that older house
on which these days have quarried and made levies.
For Memory is the wind's voice in the crevice,
a wild song through those stones and in the boughs
of trees fast-dug in flint-chips of the novice;
it is the count of hooves for ever dinned
in the ears of the world by the hard-ridden wind;
and more than these and more than headlong haste
of events galloping through widening waste
into the cumulative past—to keep
galloping on with never pause nor sleep—
it is the past itself, the dead time's will
poisoning today's pulse and potent still;
it is the ruled heart's heritage, mortmain;
darkness it is and talons of the rain.

And under earth, so varied and so golden
telling must halt, lie jars which life's old trouble
brimmed gaily, which have felt that wine embolden
hopes that looked out on many a morning olden.
And were they dupes of the dawn, then, seeing double,
since all are smashed, the false clay like the noble,
knaves and brave men all gone, and dainty wenches?
Not, surely, while the grape yet spurts one bubble,
though vessels crack and are pushed down from their benches.
And these that there lie shattered, and their nights,
rapturous, and their days, or meek as prayer,
or polished like hard brass by glinting lights,
fell, each, before some fumbling hour, their slayer.
Now is the spread stain of their deaths long vanished
and the wine froths again and never gayer,
though theirs is all soaked up, dank earth replenished,
so it might seem the book closed, the tale finished;
yet are they loot of Memory, who comes
unrecognised from rifling those bleak tombs. . . .
Stranger at the door, like doom, disaster,
no man can bar you out, this house's master.

·   ·   ·   ·   ·   ·

In our own garments left to face the drear
whinings of winter, stripped of gauds and gear
save what is patently our due and worn
by rights inherent, cold indeed were morn,
naked were noon. No comfort could we claim
except from that one wavering inward flame
unquenched through change and time, which though it wrought
in intricate iron the twisted chain of thought,
link by link stretching, vagrantly designed,
back past first hammerings of conscious mind,
is yet so fine, for all its intense white core,
stretched fingers freeze which were but chilled before.

(Strange miracle of self, mysterious, lit
no man knows how nor whence uprises it!
Lamp by lamp flickers out; this flame burns on
here—yet remotely here—and ever alone,
freezing and powerless, too, for each isled spark
were little avail against the encroaching dark
and life would perish on its pavement-flags
but that we clasp about us cast-off rags
and robes of dead kings. . . .)
                                    Rain over the world:
one handspan counts a million splashes hurled
minute by tireless minute; yet these are
random and wayward only, scattering far.
Denser, outnumbering the raindrop prisms,
there's a dumb deluge driven across night's chasms,
hard in upon us, unresisted, beating
our lives to patterns imposed past all defeating
by our poor wills; we are storm-carried, storm-shed,
battered by streaming multitudes of these dead.

They are about us on all sides: the dust
is restless; the bruised tongues of trodden weeds
speak with harsh voices, menace; grass-blades thrust
at parrying air that mirrors bygone deeds;
and who might think the unquiet is, at most,
wistful backgazing of the unbodied host,
homesick for life, who tread some screened-off path
of supernatural being beyond death,

31

let him once clutch at his own arms, so trussed
in thongs of old inheritance they can
but move in those accustomed tasks of man
allotted, limited, by the flesh they wear
ancestrally; he'll find an answer there,
fragile for sure, yet tougher than a ghost.

Indeed, we are the substance of their thought
which starves in air, can balance on no mystic
knife-edge of abstract being, twixt nought and nought,
so kneads itself in this inert, this plastic
material of our lives. But reckoning so,
farther and farther back, bared long-ago
which spores in shafts of time and mushroom-swells
through midnight-centuries, sees all things else
not as existence, but as forms worked over
in one huge bulk ere each is lost for ever,
not as reality but its escape
in impress after impress of pure shape,
and so dissolves the world. Now only appear
re-shuffling motion and the turn of the year:
all is become sheer action which perceives
bright leaves themselves as rustling of the leaves,
the bird's flight as the bird. This, heart denies
eternally; and Memory, too, replies—
links up the many flights upon one thread
of keen-eyed bird too busy to be dead
between flights done; for Memory stays the hour
and behind flower-growth is even the flower.
And we ourselves are Memory, and retain
so much of those gone, the little death can gain
is found a cheat of the senses; change and birth
convulsive writhings of autophagous earth.

· · · · · ·

Argument is the blade-bright window-pane
which shears off cleanly the slant sheaf of rain,
and in the room heart's dream and life's desire
are radiance and curled, unfolding fire.
Here thought may ponder in peace or work at will
or take down book from shelf and read his fill;

but though among men's assets he bides long
always his ears are tuned on that same song
of rain outside; for that's the force he knew
which drenched his hands that battled it, breaking through,
while yet he was homeless in the world, unsafe,
wandering in mindless marshes the wind's waif,
and had not learned to build up words and fix
a house for himself in speech's bonded bricks.
Hearing it he remembers: though large walls
shelter him now, hold out the rain, rain falls.

And ever the untaught earth, comrade of yore,
out there under the dark and dripping leaves,
although its slave-bent back, laid bare, receives
whip-stripes of rain, possesses yet that more,
wisdom and fullness, which thought has not known,
never can reach. For earth, stooped labourer,
treading the furrow of seasons, early astir
and late abed from heavy fields, wild sown,
has wind and sun for sure realities,
endures this lash, too, as a thing plain-shown,
simple as flooded rivers, tumbling seas,
gaunt hills across the sky. . . . These are earth's own;
but thought has only sounds and shadows thrown
by hollow powers, obscure immensities,
upon the screen called living. And the good, solid
meat that earth munches, truth, is proved invalid;
thought is unfed—and even thought has grown
a trifle impatient of philosophies. . . .

And mourns, like Memory, old simplicities,
other truth yet, as stark as in years younger
trod the wet clay—till this plain truth of hunger
cries: 'Time to rouse! Put by the reading-glass
which showed up print so clearly, a jagged mass
of black rocks in a dangerous foam of white,
showed more than sight could know, but not like sight,
split into jutting patches the blunt sense
and took more note of blots than eloquence.
Time now to trust our eyes, which if they find
less than the glass, less than contents the mind,

have yet their own sure knowledge of shape and fact
not as things purely are, but as they act.
And well to go among men, see how they do
the will of the past and bend their backs thereto,
the past that guides them, rules them, flogs—and flings
a despot's largesse, treasure of spoiled kings.
See how they walk between a day and a day,
command the future, and the past obey,
their present only a footing on some height
that fronts new dawn for ever, dazed with light;
see how their knowledge, between night and night,
asks, but not answers, whither winds the way.'

. . . . . .

If, as may seem, fair future spreads unfurrowed
beneath new morning and there writhes and wheels,
a sun-blind sea all silverly tomorrowed,
ruffled by promise and uncut by keels,
and, Dampiers of this dawn, we pull the prow
off-wind and pay out sheet, none tells us now
what bides our choice or if we drown or starve;
and even if the luck holds and we carve
new coasts on gaping latitudes, who traces
the scarless wake of an adventurer, lost,
sows wheat, finds gold, where we found desert places,
gashes with screws wide lanes where, lone, we crossed?

This hour, a gulp in the long throat of the past,
swallows what once was future, but soon spent;
this hour is a touch of hands, an accident
of instants meeting in unechoing vast:
it is a rail that bursts before the flourish
of black manes and time's haste; it fails our need—
now must decision be brief, must jump or perish
under the feet and fury of stampede.
And to this difficult present will succeed
what present, to be lost as this is lost?
for any decision may fall undermost,
and no hand counts the grandsons of its deed.
Foresight is but a bargain that we make,
which, even should life keep it, death will break.

. . . . . .

Who sees this time all edged about with wars
like tiny points of fire along the rim,
stretching to suns then sinking back to stars,
must hold heart-close his love to speak for him
and be his challenge to those rigorous teeth
that devour all, the answer of his faith—
which is towards the green-burst of new spring,
leaf-revelry and flower-strewn roistering,
life-joy and the dear miracle of increase.
Yet who stares forward through the shimmer of peace,
noon-heavy over valleys soaked in health,
and, baulked of sight beyond this burgeoning wealth,
finds only tremor-tapestry, hung haze,
will watch, adread, for the first beaconing blaze.
Or if the only smokes that, serpentine,
encoil the land be stubble-fires that twine
ribbons of incense round a harvest-feast,
still must one fear be troublous, one at least—
a vision of changed scene wherein smokes, black,
crawl venomous from a Gorgon chimney-stack,
with, deep below, all foreign to our ken,
strange engines and strange customs and strange men!
Well might our senses shudder when flesh hears
the coming Unseen, the spectre-march of years;
for though a man face fortunes horror-haunted,
gruesome with prophecies, and grin undaunted,
shall he bear blame from the accusing eyes
of legions grey with agony? bear their cries
sinking in floods of fire he dreams not of
and has condemned them to in very love?
Well may he see his children, such a one,
and groan doubt-drunkenly: 'What have I done?'

Rain in the clean sun falling—riches of rain
wash out the dusty fear, the air's dull stain;
ay, Memory is a shower of gilded darts
which pins today's delight on our healed hearts,
or, in our hands, is mintage of bright faith:
shame on us to be beggared by a wraith!
Now, till this trove be gone, the last coin sped,
doubt were a glum ingratitude to the dead.

How should we hold us from wild enterprise,
who use the limbs of the past and its quick eyes
and are eternally in debt to those
who stung into the earth-dawn's turgid throes
urge of keen life? We'll crash the trestles down
that barricade clear laughter, take the town
on a burst of shouting that through fissures rent
cascades its fervid glee, magnificent.
We'll slit gloom's gullet, oracling defeat,
and crack great barrels of song in open street,
free for the drinking. We'll make fabulous
this world, in honour of them who gave it us,
not just the Nelsons, Newtons, of our race,
the Phillips grounding at a landing-place
continent-wide, but all whom violence of mind,
violence of action, gave such singleness
that if they did but grow, ambitionless
except to live in the sun, they served their kind
with that straight growth of will which bears for seed
zest to create; which, grasping at blind air,
graves flowers from veriest nothing and makes fair
all that we have. Theirs was that splendid greed,
hewer of men and vineyards, nation-maker,
destroyer of hate and weakness, tyrant-breaker,
whose slow attrition, whetstone of advance,
grinds laws, arts, customs, from steel circumstance.

Then knot this hour's activity as a rope
in strength of climbing hands; for still our hope
best clings to shoulders swarming—from the mouth,
black-gaping, of loss and failure; all we know
is this jerked ladder of change whereby men go
with gasping struggle, vigour of movement—up!
Wherefore all good is effort, and all truth
encounter and overcoming. . . .

                          We whose scope
clasps the tremendous leagues of summer-south,
thunder-oppressive with curbed energies,
least of all folk need question our day's worth
or think its turmoil twitchings of spent earth.

Here noon above burnt, bony ridges hung
nerve-tense, is strident with an unheard tongue,
pregnant with daring and with destinies;
and the mist-floating islands and raw seas
nigh us and those strained ranks of shores far-swelling
knit us with fortunes idle the foretelling.
And though we plan and make, for we would keep
won soil a little beyond the ruptured sleep
of bursting tomorrows gonged upon our ears,
it is little to hold this land star-counted years
or even tonight yield it; much that fever
pounds along resolute limbs its scorching river—
doings, upheavals—much that skies, bow-drawn,
are tautened by red-eyed but still tireless dawn. . . .

Whatever the task, it lies in front: we must
build upward though we guess not to what skies,
and though the eruptive Babels that we thrust
vital in air will fritter back to dust;
else we betray the lamp behind our eyes,
the quickening in our veins, both held in trust
since long before the scumming of the germ
upon first seas. We will serve out our term:
not yet the impetus flags whose course began
when at the blank mouth of our stinking lair
we saw night's infinite curtain shake with grey,
and so went forth determined to be Man,
standing at last erect, and watched new day
wrap back the dark and strip the valley bare.

So, should our best work fail us, walls we planned
stifle in years blown over fine like sand,
or life itself reach gulfs and lorn extremes—
even some crag of ending—where bled dreams
kite in the wind weightless and the past
unclaws our very world, lets go at last,
but still remains, being Memory, one live link
of gone with all-to-come, and from the brink
peers out beyond; then, launched above that steep,
venture shall cant bold wings and with their sweep
splinter such clogging silence as they met
in older abyss where time slept stirless yet.

THE INCARNATION OF SIRIUS

In that age, the great anagram of God
Had bayed the planets from the rounds they trod,
And gathered the fixed stars in a shining nation
Like restless birds that flock before migration.

For the millennial instinct of new flight
Resolved the antinomy that fixed their light;
And, echoing in the troubled soul of Earth,
Quickened a virgin's womb, to bring to birth

What scarce was human: a rude avatar
That glistened with the enclosed wrath of a star.
The woman died in pangs, before she had kissed
The monstrous form of God's antagonist.

But at its showing forth, the poets cried
In a strange tongue; hot mouths prophesied
The coolness of the bloody vintage-drops:
'Let us be drunk at least, when the world stops!'

Anubis-headed, the heresiarch
Sprang to a height, fire-sinewed in the dark,
And his ten fingers, bracketed on high,
Were a blazing candelabra in the sky.

The desert lion antiphonally roared;
The tiger's sinews quivered like a chord;
Man smelt the blood beneath his brother's skin
And in a loving hate the sword went in.

And then the vision sank, bloody and aborted.
The stars that with rebellion had consorted
Fled back in silence to their former stations.
Over the giant face of dreaming nations

The centuries-thick coverlet was drawn.
Upon the huddled breast Aldebaran
Still glittered with its sad alternate fire:
Blue as of memory, red as of desire.

THE FACE OF THE WATERS

ONCE again the scurry of feet—those myriads
crossing the black granite; and again
laughter cruelly in pursuit; and then
the twang like a harpstring or the spring of a trap,
and the swerve on the polished surface: the soft little
    pads
sidling and skidding and avoiding; but soon caught up
in the hand of laughter and put back. . . .

There is no release from the rack
of darkness for the unformed shape,
the unexisting thought
stretched half-and-half
in the shadow of beginning and that denser black
under the imminence of huge pylons—
the deeper nought;
but neither is there anything to escape,
or to laugh,
or to twang that string which is not a string but silence
plucked at the heart of silence.

Nor can there be a floor to the bottomless;
except in so far as conjecture must arrive
lungs cracking, at the depth of its dive;
where downward further is further distress
with no change in it; as if a mile and an inch
are equally squeezed into a pinch,
and retreating limits of cold mind
frozen, smoothed, defined.

Out of the tension of silence (the twanged string);
from the agony of not being (that terrible laughter
tortured by darkness); out of it all
once again the tentative migration; once again
a universe on the edge of being born:
feet running fearfully out of nothing
at the core of nothing:
colour, light, life, fearfully
becoming eyes and understanding: sound becoming
    ears. . . .

For eternity is not space reaching
on without end to it; not time without end to it,
nor infinity working round in a circle;
but a placeless dot enclosing nothing,
the pre-time pinpoint of impossible beginning,
enclosed by nothing, not even by emptiness—
impossible: so wholly at odds with possibilities
that, always emergent and wrestling and inter-linking,
they shatter it and return to it, are all of it and part of it.
It is your hand stretched out to touch your neighbour's,
and feet running through the dark, directionless like darkness.

Worlds that were spun adrift re-enter
that intolerable centre;
indeed the widest-looping comet
never departed from it;
it alone exists.
And though, opposing it, there persists
the enormous structure of forces, laws,
as background for other coming and going,
that's but a pattern, a phase, no pause,
of ever-being-erected, ever-growing
ideas unphysically alternative
to nothing, which is the quick. You may say hills live,
or life's the imperfect aspect of a flowing
that sorts itself as hills; much as thoughts wind
selectively through mind.

The eggshell collapses
in the fist of the eternal instant;
all is what it was before.
Yet is that eternal instant
the pinpoint bursting into reality,
the possibilities and perhapses,
the feet scurrying on the floor.
It is the suspense also
with which the outward thrust
holds the inward surrender—
the stresses in the shell before it buckles under:
the struggle to magpie-morning and all life's clamour and lust;
the part breaking through the whole;
light and the clear day and so simple a goal.

THE EARTH

MINUTE made visible and heard,
  Fact born of space by lust of time,
The aftermath of the first word,
  Mote dried from a drift of slime;

Earth, 'tis enough to know but this,
  You give such beauty to our eyes
And all our senses, here love is
  And the dream-stuff of Paradise.

Your rise in night and your decline
  Sentries nor scientists behold,
No lovers pray of you divine
  Heat for a loved one's heart grown cold.

Yet in illimitable law
  Guessed at by symbols, you may be
Lovely as Venus whom you saw
  This night above your darkening sea.

And where a world has come alive
  May not your littleness be host,
Food of the spirit, the soul's hive,
  Home and haven of Holy Ghost?

AUTUMN
(from R. M. Rilke)

HEART, it is time. The fruitful summer yields;
The shadows fall across the figured dial,
The winds are loosed upon the harvest fields.
See that these last fruits swell upon the vine;
Grant them as yet a southern day or two
Then press them to fulfilment, and pursue
The last of sweetness in the heavy wine.

You shall be homeless, shall not build this year.
You shall be solitary and long alone;
Shall wake, and read, and write long letters home,
And on deserted pavements here and there
Shall wander restless, as the leaves are blown.

THE GRAND CORTÈGE

THE grand cortège of glory and youth is gone,
flaunt standards, and the flood of brazen tone:
I alone linger, a regretful guest,
here where the hostelry has crumbled down,
emptied of warmth and life, and the little town
lies cold and ruin'd, all its bravery done,
wind-blown, wind-blown, where not even dust may rest.
No cymbal-clash warms the chill air: the way
lies stretch'd beneath a slanting afternoon,
the which no piled pyres of the slaughter'd sun,
no silver sheen of eve shall follow: Day,
ta'en at the throat and choked, in the huge slum
o' the common world, shall fall across the coast,
yellow and bloodless, not a wound to boast.
But if this bare-blown waste refuse me home
and if the skies wither my vesper-flight,
'twere well to creep, or ever livid night
wrap the disquiet earth in horror, back
where the old church stands on our morning's track,
and in the iron-entrellis'd choir, among
rust tombs and blazons, where an isle of light
is bosom'd in the friendly gloom, devise
proud anthems in a long forgotten tongue:
so cozening youth's despair o'er joy that dies.

THE PROTAGONIST

No sleep! I rise and burn the night away.
Swift through the open window drives a moth—
and stages yet another Passion Play.

The candle flares—a Star is in the east.
The altar's lit for sacrifice afresh,
the dance of death and ecstasy, the feast,
more bread than wine, of bloodless insect flesh.

Sudden, the reckless Dionysian whirl
is ended in a headlong plummet dive—
Descended into Hell—Now mark the curl,
the crisped and singed antennae ends contrive.
The devotee aswoon, as in the grave,
lies two untroubled seconds. Then, it stirs—
He rose the third day—see, the struggle brave
resumes—the palsied wing yet feebly whirrs!
The painful upward crawl that gathers strength
and speed betimes—*ascended into Heaven*—
the pause in ecstasy, a thumbnail's length
below the Flame, the quickening flesh to leaven
at Life's own Source . . . *He sitteth at the right
hand of*—that beauteous, quivering naked Gleam.
Desires resurge. So keen the new delight,
all the old scorching pain becomes a dream:
the insistent Present calls; the Past forgot,
once more the Living Bread prepares the Feast;
the Hero-victim reenacts the Plot—
the candle flares. A Star is in the east.

SLEEP

Do you give yourself to me utterly,
  Body and no-body, flesh and no-flesh,
Not as a fugitive, blindly or bitterly,
  But as a child might, with no other wish?
Yes, utterly.

Then I shall bear you down my estuary,
Carry you and ferry you to burial mysteriously,
Take you and receive you,
Consume you, engulf you,
In the huge cave, my belly, lave you
With huger waves continually.

And you shall cling and clamber there
And slumber there, in that dumb chamber,
Beat with my blood's beat, hear my heart move
Blindly in bones that ride above you,
Delve in my flesh, dissolved and bedded,
Through viewless valves embodied so—

Till daylight, the expulsion and awakening,
  The riving and the driving forth,
Life with remorseless forceps beckoning—
  Pangs and betrayal of harsh birth.

THE POINT OF NOON

THE point of noon is past, outside: light is asleep;
brooding upon its perfect hour: the woods are deep
and solemn, fill'd with unseen presences of light
that glint, allure, and hide them; ever yet more bright
(it seems) the turn of a path will show them: nay, but rest;
seek not, and think not; dream, and know not; this is best:
the hour is full; be lost: whispering, the woods are bent,
This is the only revelation; be content.

AFFINITY

I WONDER if the cabbage knows
He is less lovely than the rose,
Or if he squats in snug content,
A source of noble nourishment.
And if he pities for her sins
The rose, who has no vitamins,
Or, if one thing his green heart knows . . .
That same Fire that warms the rose.

TURN TO THE GRASS

TURN to the grass
And put away fears;
Over earth it marches
With its thin green spears;
Yet where it goes
River never flows
Wider than its army
Of thin green spears.

Turn to the grass
And put away tears;
The grass knows no leader
No captain to its spears;
Yet where it goes
Plough never ploughs
Wider than its army
Of thin green spears.

Turn to the grass
And put away grief;
The grass is not fearful
Its swords are in sheaf;
Lovely are its swords
And its spears towards heaven;
Loveliest of all
In the low sun of even.

Praise God for the grass
That covers up tears,
Marching through the land
With its thin green spears.

THE BARRIER

I LAY face-downward on the grass
Listening for the Earth's heart-beats;
And I heard
The broken echoes of my own—
And, in my own, of all men's.

I came upon a water-pool
At the foot of a leaning gum-tree;
The sky was in it,
And the motionless branches of the gum-tree.

With steadying hand upon the bole
I, too, leaned over;
And there in the still water I saw
The hates and loves of the unquiet souls
Of all men,
And the pool was become unrestful,
Though not a whiff of air had ruffled it.

I drew back shamefastly,
And, from a little distance, saw
The mother-quiet nestle down again.
And so it is—always!
The consciousness of being
Is like a barrier round about us,
A barrier we may neither breach nor overpass.

THE REAPER

UNDER the dying sun
  And the moon's frail shell,
The fields are clear as glass:
  I love them well.

A horse's amber flanks
  Shine in the grain.
The wheel of the reaper cleaves
  A yellow lane.

The reaper is ruddy gold,
  Unearthly bright,
Driving an amber cloud,
  Touched with its light.

They say the earth's a stone
  Wrinkled and old,
Yet she has steeds of fire
  And men of gold!

COCKEREL SUN

This golden cockerel summer sun ruffles his feathers into sleep,
While from the woods about him spread, the foxes of the
evening creep

And move like soft and fluent winds before his dwelling shut
and barred
(For Time has drawn his bolt against a chance intruder in the
yard).

And now he dreams, bright beak beneath the cloudy darkness
of his wing
And sees about him suns and moons whirling in one tremendous
ring.

Too light, too bright the spinning white his sleeping vision gives
delight
Under his eyelid stretched against the dark reality of night.

Till gradually, his dream grown thin, waking, the foxes stealthy
gone,
The cockerel crows and spreads his wings, transcending earth—
the rising sun.

THE BIRDS GO BY

WESTWARD at even . . . yet never, never to die!
Surely they live as ever the laugh and the sigh:
After the fight and the fall, the defeat of the pilgrim,
    The birds go by.

No, not for dying like all the sweet flowers are they,
—Flowers giving hope to mankind on their little stay,
Failing only as love fails at the end of the day.

Green earth and water have gladdening out of their cry,
Lifting the eyes of the heart to the height of the sky:
I dream that they bear to the dead the thoughts of the living . . .
    The birds go by.

From SWANS AT NIGHT

WITHIN the night, above the dark,
　I heard a host upon the air,
Upon the void they made no mark,
　For all that they went sailing there.

And from that host there came a cry,
　A note of calling strange and high;
I heard it blown against the sky,
　Till naught there seemed but it and I.

A long and lonely wraith of sound,
　It floated out in distance wide,
As though it knew another bound,
　A space wherein it never died.

I heard the swans, I heard the swans,
　I heard the swans that speed by night;
That ever, where the starlight wans,
　Fly on unseen within the height.

I never knew how wide the dark,
　I never knew the depth of space,
I never knew how frail a bark,
　How small is man within his place,

Not till I heard the swans go by,
　Not till I marked their haunting cry,
Not till, within the vague on high,
　I watched them pass across the sky. . . .

E

THE LOVE OF SWANS

THE two swans break
The silver slumber of the lake;
White tipped their beaks are set
Scarlet upon jet;
Wider flow the ripples from
Their high and ornate sterns
And like galleons they come
Where the sun's reflection burns
Upon the gleaming gloom
And where so very still is
The opening of the water lilies.
Glad am I my life should be
Of this the repository;
In some future's clime
A spirit in search of plunder
In the debris of old time
Will gasp with joy and wonder,
Finding the treasure trove
Of these birds' love.

REGENT-BIRD AND GIRL

THE gold and black regent-bird
Flashes into the lantana
Among a swarm of flowers.
Bright bird, gay thicket of flowers.
A girl sits on a log across a waterfall,
Sings to the bower-bird among the flowers.
She swings her feet over the log
Splashes the water-brink with her toes.
She makes a singing-sound, as the stream.
She looks up to the blue and green mosaic
Of sky between the piccabean palms.
A whip-bird swishes the cool silence.
A red leaf falls, zigzags from a vine
Interlacing the rain-forest giants.
The girl watches the falling leaf,
Tries to imitate the whip-bird.
Water-beetles skim an eddying pool,
A crayfish edges round a pebble.
The red leaf falls to the water, is swept
Over the cascade, a spinning disk.
The air is cool in the gully,
The sun warm on the breasts of the girl.

And the regent-bird looks at the golden girl
And thinks of nothing but berries.

THE HERON

THE crested heron flies over the lake,
Lower and lower falling with down-stretched legs
Slanting to the waiting water; she touches,
And starts ripples in widening circles, like water-lilies
Unrolling their edges and staring at the sun.

She sits the water as a queen enthroned in light;
She drifts in hyacinths, purple and yellow, and ivory;
She sails magnolia open, swayed by wind puffs
That idle with her steering; her pink feet hidden
And lazing pleasurably in the limpid lake.

She takes the wind puffs in her fan, and with twisted neck
Plunges her golden beak, wet first with dipping,
Amongst her plumes, and vainly combs her white;
Bewitching as a maiden négligée,
The crested heron unselfconsciously, serenely preens.

She takes her time; why haste on such a day?
She lifts her wings to let the warm sun pierce,
She rocks herself to wet her lovely sides
Till not an inch of all her loveliness is dry,
And the reeds look on, murmuring of their visitor.

Now she stays her burnished beak, for she has done;
She arches her neck and, knowing well her beauty,
Looks at her gleaming image in the water mirror,
And with a heavy lift of sodden wings, lifts up
Her wonder, and leaves the empty lake.

A FLIGHT OF WILD GEESE

Wu Tao-tzŭ, the greatest of Chinese artists, was once com-
missioned by the Emperor Ming Huang of the T'ang Dynasty
to paint a landscape-roll. Wu so entered into the spirit of the
scene, that he could walk about in the picture at will. One day
he wandered over a distant mountain, and was never seen again.

Now Wu Tao-tzŭ, continuing his stroll
Into the landscape on the silken roll,
Comes to the misty shores around a sheet
Of broad water, reaching from his feet
To where a promontory's rocky bar
Lies in the evening sky, it is so far.
Their taper necks stretched out in line of flight,
The wild geese row over at a height;
And while they clang their long-throated cry,
Tow the full moon into an autumn sky.
Diagonals that widen from a wake
Lattice the tranquil surface of the lake
When in the lapping ebb they intervene,
And shake the level creases of its sheen:
A clear grey-green, and yet with depth opaque;
As though four ladies rolling silk should take
Layer on layer of green silk, and of grey,
And stretch them taut across a vacant bay.

To skirt these shores, the painter has to pass
Where the long legs of flowering river-grass
Stand in the margin shallows: feathery rushes
Drawn by his most meticulous of brushes,
Their tufted tops with seed are light and loose
As the soft underdown of a grey goose.
In a flat inlet hereabouts, he sees
How, warily protruding out of these,
A narrow black prow nuzzles the bank:
The grasses thriving here are lush and lank.
Lulled by the idle suction of the tide,
And the slap of lapsing water against the side,
The wily poet snoozing in the stern
With chin on elbow, smiles in unconcern
As round his line a school of mullet feeds.

Under an overcoat of plaited reeds,
He wears the faded purple robe he wore;
To shade his head, a limpet made of straw.
His scant beard and moustaches' straggling hair
Are lightly lifted; flow along the air
Like water-weed that sways this way and that;
And the two fish-tailed ribbons from his hat
Follow them, flapping with a fugal motion.

To bait this odd angler is the notion
The artist forms, for judging by his creel,
Necessity will be his evening meal.

Wu Tao-tzŭ:
'Among the Hundred Surnames, mine is Wu.
Pardon my mannerless presumption, who,
Ancient and solitary one, are you?'

The rustic archly opens up one eye
To view this doze-disturbing stranger by;
Yawns like a fox, and stretches to arouse
His cramped limbs from their pictorial drowse.

The Old Fisherman:
'I came here twenty years ago or more,
And yet these hands have never once before
Shaken themselves in salutation's hold.
Then I was Chang Chih-ho. But now the Old
Fisherman of the Waters and the Mists
Conveys of what my way of life consists.'

Wu Tao-tzŭ:
'Why did you quit humanity and home
And choose this wilderness in which to roam?
Why in a humble sampan hold aloof,
Its wicker cradle as your only roof?'

Chang Chih-ho:
'I find it serves quite well to keep me dry.
After the autumn rains stop, and the sky
Clears rapidly, all space shall cover me.

The moonrise, pale and golden, on the sea
Fulfils my modest wishes for a door;
And the sea's jade pavement lays the floor.
These, with the valley walls, make up my home.
What do you mean by saying that I roam?
Here cares and creditors no more infest
The house of mind. Its poverty is rest.
Possessing nothing, I am not possessed.
The State's a monstrous and amorphous plan,
Man's mobilized insanity, and man
Believes it real. Afraid of being free,
He fights to keep the cangue, and cannot flee.
An intimate I would far rather be
Of the white gull which climbs and squalls aloud
Sailing across that black cliff of cloud,
Than have the freedom of my spirit furled
And flung upon the dust-heap of the world.'

Wu Tao-tzŭ:
'From vanity of rank you may retire;
The lust to rule, that menial desire,
The web of power, possessions which degrade—
These you may shun: you cannot thus evade
Your unlived life, the fate you left unpaid.'

Chang Chih-ho:
'No debts or duties did I set aside;
And one who under Su Tsung occupied
The post of minister, was no misfit:
I fled not from the world, but into it.
What other, pray, could I escape to? I'm
Still in this world. I've been here all the time.'

Wu Tao-tzŭ:
'Go where you will, you take your troubled mind,
Whose fears you cannot face, nor leave behind.
In vain your doubts and sorrows you suppress;
In vain avoid society's distress:
Escape has no road from its loneliness.'

Chang Chih-ho:
'An Emperor's entreaty I would spurn;
I have no inclination to return
To where the simple way is smothered in
The court's incessant fuss; where dust and din
Cover the capital, as with a pall;
Where I could have no peace of mind at all.
The case of Chuang Tzŭ doubtless you recall?
Two high officials from the State of Ch'u,
Who called upon him for an interview,
While he was fishing in the river P'u,
Announced, "Our Prince proposes to transfer
The government to you—an office, sir,
Only your wisdom can administer."
The Taoist did not deign to turn his head.
With rod in hand, he watched his line and said,
"In Ch'u there is a tortoise which they hold
Sacred for divination, so I'm told.
It has been dead three thousand years, and since
Kept in a covered casket by the Prince,
Who heats its shell in his ancestral shrine
And reads the cracks in order to divine.
Given the choice when caught, which would it choose:
To stay alive, draggling its tail in ooze;
Or to be reverenced by men, but dead?"
"To be alive, of course," the officials said.
"Off with you then, and let me," he replied,
"Waggle my tail, too, in the muddy tide."
And some declare the sage washed out his ears
To cleanse them of political ideas;
And that downstream a cowherd then complained
The waters were polluted and profaned.'

Wu Tao-tzŭ:
'But see! The skeins of geese arriving span
The sky and write the words for "one" and "man".'

Chang Chih-ho:
'And yet they have been here since time began.'

60

Down the sky in file the wild geese tack,
Slanting their obliquely angled track
Toward the estuary's bank of sand
With blocks of basalt strewn along the strand.
The leader there comes skidding in, to sit
On a long splash, for the sheer sport of it:
His tail-feathers fan to brake the flight;
And webbed feet and red legs alight,
As if fixed in a clear aquamarine,
So still the surface water is, and green.
There he stands upright in the water-rings,
Throws out his breast, and flaps his wide wings;
There ducks, to ladle over back and head
Wingfuls of water; shakes his tail to shed
Superfluous drops; and washing over, grooms
Down smooth and trim his toilet-ruffled plumes;
And then into a comfortable unrest
Worries the pin-plumage of his breast.
More glide in after him. The others land
Pinions aloft, and settle on the sand,
Where flat snapping bills hiss and contest
Scraps of aquatic weed that one possessed.
Pushing a fold of glass against the stream,
One paddles in pursuit of his own gleam.
Another stoops his pliant neck to sip
This running ripple with the glassy lip,
And elevates it after every dip.
A third, whose bill tugged at the wavering weeds,
Lifts their dripping ribbons up, and feeds.
Riding its undulating ebb, the fleet
Of geese sets sail upon the glaucous sheet;
But a snapped stick startles one among
Them. Instantly the floating flock is sprung.
Low over the water skims each pair:
The downbeat of the wing-tip in the air
Touching the upbeat of its image there.
Once in the central air, they travel south
Beyond the sandspit at the river's mouth,
Beyond the dim horizon. All are gone.
But, like a flock of feathers dropped upon
The refluent air after their motion's flown,

61

A soft flocculence of cloud is strown;
And hovers, as invisible waves of wake
Diverge, and on the mountains sprayless break.

Wu Tao-tzŭ:
'They have migrated to a warmer clime.'

Chang Chih-ho:
'They will be here now till the end of time.'

A light breeze that springs up off the bay,
Bending the plumed grasses all one way
And carrying their seeded fluff astray,
Just as suddenly drops. At once the rushes'
Thicket of dry whispers thins and hushes
To a faint rustle. Nothing stirs the brake.
Chang winds his fishing-line in from the lake.

Wu's face is lost in an astonished look,
For from it dangles neither bait nor hook!

Wu Tao-tzŭ:
'How ever do you hope to catch a stray
Tadpole, though you angle here all day?
This is no way to get a bite. You need
An iron hook, a juicy worm or weed
For bait, with float and sinker, if you wish
To offer some enticement to a fish.'

Hinting that he knows more than one would think,
The artful Taoist slyly tips a wink:

Chang Chih-ho:
'Ah! But that's not what I was fishing for!'

He poles his lean punt away from shore.
The layered strands of vapour closing in,
Leave no trace that he has ever been. . . .

Into infinite distance, sad and clear,
Recede the miles of autumn atmosphere:

With pale citrine tone, the watery light
That shines out after rain, washes their height.
The autumn mountain, swept as neat and clean
As the tidy winds can, reclines serene:
No twig is out of place; no leaf is seen
Of all that tarnished ruin of gold which lay
Underfoot so densely, yesterday.
The earth has claimed their tribute to decay.
Upon its sides the naked forests brood,
Locked in a crystalline disquietude;
And looped with sleeping vines and beards of moss,
Despair for want of leaves, the season's loss.
Each tall, gaunt, calligraphic tree
Forked against the light's sour clarity,
Soars with static branches, sparse and bare,
In the remote and disappointed air.
An empty vast, the autumn waters lie
Merging into the open sea of sky.
Slowly the ebb goes out, and from the height
Drains away the westering tide of light.

Ah! The evening's mood is growing late.
The peasant enters now his brushwood gate.
The garden overgrown with grass and weed,
Where spires of wild lettuce run to seed,
Lies drenched with recent rain, and desolate.
A sulphur-coloured butterfly chases its mate
Over the fence with devious flutterings:
They are the only autumn leaves with wings.
The altered air that chills the end of day
Makes the fishing-nets and tackle sway
Gently over on their bamboo poles.
And now a village bell remotely tolls
The still and solemn hour; now holds its peace.
The work of men, the year's affairs decrease.
Now lamps are lit in windows far and near.
See! Through the yellow dusk their flames appear.
Within the peasant's hut two suppers wait.
Ah! The evening's mood is growing late.

A smooth moon in the laminated fog
That weaves the stagnant levels of a bog
With trails of gossamer, is hanging low
Its pallid disc, too early yet to glow.
Beside this languid marsh the artist walks.
Still to the withered old lotus stalks
The rattling seeds in conic pods adhere;
The flounced leaves float, tattered and sere;
And sere the willow leaves spin as they sift
On a despondent pond their falling drift.
There like sallow sampans they are thrust
Aimlessly along by a tired gust
Into a backwater. There some dust
Is spent, and settles, and the waste becalms
Among an undergrowth of roots with arms
For now the world of nature is subdued
And grave with an autumnal lassitude.

Out on the lake a solitary sail
Goes home into the world. With this detail
The subtle Taoist in his fishing-smack
Sketches in the landscape's only lack.
Its blind of white grows smaller, outward blown.
One last goose wings on its way alone:
A hook of ink against the silken sky,
Gone with the echo of a far high cry. . . .

   Wu Tao-tzŭ:
'A lone goose and a lone sail depart:
They do not leave the shore, they leave the heart.'

A WORD FOR THE INNKEEPER

No luck, there's no room here.
There's not a corner of the yard
but has them sleeping packed
as close as pigeons in a market coop.
I'd not refuse you did I have a spot
where you could even seat yourself and wife.
Look for yourself—baggage and camels, and men,
women and kids—a rowdy, thieving mob,
sprawled everywhere. Now, are you satisfied?
In all my twenty years of keeping inns
I've never seen the like before.
Such avalanche of flesh, such herds of humans!
All day long for days
they've drifted in, mud to the knees,
with blistered feet, fagged, and empty-bellied.
They've eaten the whole village out—
there's not a wineskin wet,
not a cheese remains. And bread!
My friend, the baker, fell exhausted in a tub of dough.
They found him sleeping there, a monstrous loaf!
Myself, I haven't slept these three nights past.
I daren't—they'd pinch the very doors for wood.
Well, there it is, there's nothing I can do.
The Government's to blame—
I ask you who but fools would take
a census in the wintertime?
A bitter winter too it is—
and if I *am* a weather-man—they say I am—
my father was, he knew the signs—
the shifting ants for floods, and all the rest—
I'd say the sky is full of snow.
Make on and find some shelter for your wife.
A pretty girl she is. You'll be a father soon?
God grant you, sir, a lusty son.
Let's see, let's see—two hundred yards along
you'll strike a narrow track, a cattle pad,
that branches to the right and leads
into the hills where there are caves.

At least you'll have a roof, and dung for fire—
the cattle shelter there—
but even so they're cleaner than the cattle I have here.
The wind has fallen. There's a flake of snow—
a frozen swallow, if you like poetic terms.
My father was a poet. But you must haste.
Yes, light your lantern now. The stars are
coming out. How sharp and cold they are,
like points of silvered spears! They say
a brand new star arrived the other day
but stars to me are much alike as sheep.
Goodnight, goodnight, my friend. A sound roof,
and a dry bed, and a sunny morning!
Goodnight. See you do not miss the track—
two hundred yards along, and to the right.
Goodnight.

SPACE

COLUMBUS looks towards the New World,
the sea is flat and nothing breaks the rim
of the world's disc;
he takes the sphere with him.

Day into night the same, the only change
the living variation at the core
of this man's universe;
and silent on the silver ship he broods.

Red gouts of weed, and skimming fish, to crack
the stupefying emptiness of sea,
night, and the unimpassioned gaze of stars . . .

And God be praised for the compass, oaths
bawled in the fo'c'sle,
broken heads and wine,
song and guitars,

the tramp of boots,
the wash and whip of brine.

FIFTH DAY

In William Rufus's hall the galleries reached
half to the rafters like a roost for lords,
perching the fashion of England; back seats fetched
more than a nabob's bribe. The season affords
nothing so sought as these hard boards;
so rustling ladies, crush your muslin frocks. . . .
There's Mrs Fitzherbert in the royal box.

Scarlet and ermine judges, wigs, gold laces,
canopies, woolsacks, drapings in red and green
for Peers' benches and Commons'—the culprit faces
a canvas not a court, a painted scene;
and from the obsolete frame there lean
figures trapped for tomorrow: history hooks
the observer into its foreground while he looks.

The proclamation for silence! Silence lies deep
under two hundred years. Almost you would say
the heralds are varnished over, standing asleep,
and the voice demanding silence has echoed away
far into silence. As if that day
were flat, still surface at last. But there survives
a hand in the midst, turning old thoughts, old lives.

Quill-marks migrate across a writing-block—
it is Joseph Gurney's hand. He heads his page:
'Fifth day: it wants a quarter of twelve o'clock:
the Chancellor presides'; so sets a stage
where words must jostle and engage
and die on utterance. But as they pass
paper shall catch their breaths like fog on glass.

'Warren Hastings Esquire, come forth in court
to save thee and thy bail' . . . Seven years shall run;
but a verdict will not end it—would a report
settle affairs in India, cool that sun
that policies well and ill begun
curve about since da Gama? Britain was built
round India and on Hastings—prove his guilt!

'Charges of misdemeanours and high crimes'—
prove—if proved, share them! Long ago, far hence,
they are drowned under the influx of new times.
What's done goes on for ever as consequence;
but there's some blurring of evidence
by happenings more at elbow. Why try this man?
Hastings is no concern of Pakistan.

But it concerns all men that what they do
remains significant unbroken thread
of the fabric of our living. A man spoke so,
and acted so; and everything done or said
is superseded and overlaid
by change of time and pattern. Be that as it may,
there was need he lift his finger, say his say.

Attitude matters: bearing. Action in the end
goes down the stream as motion, merges as such
with the whole of life and time; but islands stand:
dignity and distinctness that attach
to the inmost being of us each.
It matters for man's private respect that still
face differs from face and will from will.

It is important how men looked and were.
Infirm, staggering a little, as Hastings was,
his voice was steady as his eyes. Kneeling at the bar
(ruler but late of millions) had steeled his poise;
he fronted inescapable loss
and thrown, stinking malice and disrepute,
calmly, a plain man in a plain suit.

Undersized, spare, licked dry by tropic heat;
one, with severe forehead and hard lips,
who had taken age's shilling and complete
grey uniform though not its grey eclipse—
with movements like commands, like whips:
here is the centre, whether for applause or loathing,
when evidence and acquittal alike mean nothing.

F

But the eye strays from centre. The axle's part
is just to endure the play and spin of the spokes.
It is another figure rouses the heart,
a scholar loving his nation above his books,
who, pushed by a conscience that provokes
past reason or discretion, steps, half blind,
to darkness of anger from great light of his mind.

A compact, muscular man warms to the work
which will embitter him in another's feud,
his own mission and error. Edmund Burke
for right's clear sake is hounding his pursued,
inveterate, through this seven years' cloud
where subtle poison—Francis—steeps him whole;
he stands at the middle of the floor and twists his scroll.

'My lords, the gentlemen whom the Commons appoint
to manage this prosecution direct me thus
to inform your lordships' . . . The cool phrases joint
one into other, and clause links on clause
wrought arguments whereby the cause
of justice and upright dealing may extend
from Westminster to India, and beyond.

Pitt sits near Fox and the managers, listens and learns.
Burke's heavy features liven with that magic
under them and their spectacles, which turns
knowledge to vision, and vision to strategic
marshalling of words and march of logic
through illustrations like landscapes and up steep
Quebec heights of statistics. Fox is asleep.

Francis is awake—behind the mask of his face,
inscrutable . . . as Junius. 'I have found,'
Hastings had said, 'in private as in his place,
he is void of truth and honour.' But cards go round;
brilliant, elegant as unsound,
he is one to hold them craftily, lead them well;
Hastings is now his victim, Burke his tool.

70

Something is eternal in the tugging of minds
which is not in mountains or monuments maturing
through day and darkness of centuries; something that
    binds
life into tensions and balances enduring
amid flowers withering and years flowering;
whereby in the instant of contest men outlive
upshots that melt in hot hands that achieve.

The fifth day wore to its close. On his feet still,
Burke was become tired body, who was cold brain
of impersonal Accusation. Suddenly ill,
he suddenly was himself, forcing through pain
words that seemed far off and in vain—
empty things scattered about by someone else,
a child dressed up in a bob-wig, playing with shells.

That moment swallows everything, like the gulf
two hundred years are hushed in: the fatigues
that buzzed like sickness in his brain; the trial itself
which was a swarming of motives and intrigues.
All the antagonisms, leagues,
plots and pamphlets are folded up, collapse;
but still the persons move, the drama shapes.

Here is displayed failure. Though there ensues
a recovery, a tomorrow that shall atone—
another hour, when Burke's voice shall cry: 'Choose!'
and he shall stand in England almost alone,
weighing a guillotine and a throne—
results mean little; they cancel and coalesce.
A gesture will outweigh them, a trick of dress.

The common work outweighs them—the anonymous gift
to the future, living, widening. What indeed
of that old struggle matters or would be left
but for an ordinary fellow's simple need,
who had a family to feed
and liked going to church looked up to, known
as a man with a tidy business of his own?

71

Fox hurried to Burke's aid. The court adjourned.
Gurney stoppered his inkhorn, wiped his pen. . . .
Poor Mr Burke! But it was money earned
lightly and sweetened labour, for lesser men,
to go home early now and then.
Tuck today under an arm—though Hastings bent
that frown, there remained but shorthand. He bowed and
    went.

TERRA AUSTRALIS

I

CAPTAIN Quiros and Mr William Lane,
Sailing some highway shunned by trading traffic
Where in the world's skull like a moonlit brain
Flashing and crinkling rolls the vast Pacific,

Approached each other zigzag, in confusion,
Lane from the west, the Spaniard from the east,
Their flickering canvas breaking the horizon
That shuts the dead off in a wall of mist.

'Three hundred years since I set out from Lima
And off Espiritu Santo lay down and wept
Because no faith in men, no truth in islands
And still unfound the shining continent slept;

'And swore upon the Cross to come again
Though fever, thirst and mutiny stalked the seas
And poison spiders spun their webs in Spain,
And did return, and sailed three centuries,

'Staring to see the golden headlands wade
And saw no sun, no land, but this wide circle
Where moonlight clots the waves with coils of weed
And hangs like silver moss on sail and tackle,

'Until I thought to trudge till time was done
With all except my purpose run to waste;
And now upon this ocean of the moon,
A shape, a shade, a ship, and from the west!'

II

'What ship?' 'The *Royal Tar*!' 'And whither bent?'
'I seek the new Australia.' 'I, too, stranger;
Terra Australis, the great continent
That I have sought three centuries and longer;

'And westward still it lies, God knows how far,
Like a great golden cloud, unknown, untouched,
Where men shall walk at last like spirits of fire
No more by oppression chained, by sin besmirched.'

'Westward there lies a desert where the crow
Feeds upon poor men's hearts and picks their eyes;
Eastward we flee from all that wrath and woe
And Paraguay shall yet be Paradise.'

'Eastward,' said Quiros, as *San Pedro* rolled,
High-pooped and round in the belly like a barrel,
'Men tear each other's entrails out for gold;
And even here I find that men will quarrel.'

'If you are Captain Quiros you are dead.'
'The report has reached me; so is William Lane.'
The dark ships rocked together in the weed
And Quiros stroked the beard upon his chin:

'We two have run this ocean through a sieve
And though our death is scarce to be believed
Seagulls and flying-fish were all it gave
And it may be we both have been deceived.'

III

'Alas, alas, I do remember now;
In Paradise I built a house of mud
And there were fools who could not milk a cow
And idle men who would not though they could.

'There were two hundred brothers sailed this ocean
To build a New Australia in the east
And trifles of money caused the first commotion
And one small cask of liquor caused the last.

'Some had strange insects bite them, some had lust,
For wifeless men will turn to native women,
Yet who could think a world would fall in dust
And old age dream of smoke and blood and cannon

'Because three men got drunk?' 'With Indian blood
And Spanish hate that jungle reeked to Heaven;
And yet I too came once, or thought I did,
To Terra Australis, my dear western haven,

74

'And broke my gallows up in scorn of violence,
Gave land and honours, each man had his wish,
Flew saints upon the rigging, played the clarions:
Yet many there were poisoned by a fish

'And more by doubt; and so deserted Torres
And sailed, my seamen's prisoner, back to Spain.'
There was a certain likeness in the stories
And Captain Quiros stared at William Lane.

IV

Then 'Hoist the mainsail!' both the voyagers cried,
Recoiling each from each as from the devil;
'How do we know that we are truly dead
Or that the tales we tell may not be fable?

'Surely I only dreamed that one small bottle
Could blow up New Australia like a bomb?
A mutinous pilot I forebore to throttle
From Terra Australis send me demented home?

'The devil throws me up this Captain Quiros,
This William Lane, a phantom not yet born,
This Captain Quiros dead three hundred years,
To tempt me to disaster for his scorn—

'As if a blast of bony breath could wither
The trees and fountains shining in my mind,
Some traveller's tale, puffed out in moonlit weather,
Divert me from the land that I must find!

'Somewhere on earth that land of love and faith
In Labour's hands—the Virgin's—must exist,
And cannot lie behind, for there is death,
So where but in the west—but in the east?'

At that the sea of light began to dance
And plunged in sparkling brine each giddy brain;
The wind from Heaven blew both ways at once
And west went Captain Quiros, east went Lane.

THE OLD SAILOR

THE old sailor dreams of a little island
Rolling like an apple in the wide green sea,
A little island he could hold in his hand
Turn over this way and then that
Set a tree here, and there a nigger in a palm leaf hat.
He sailed all his life
Till his blood ran as salt as the sea,
His ship was his sweetheart and his wife.
And he passed many an island with no more
Than a glance at the bright white sand of the curving
    shore,
But now that the sailor is old
He would like a little island like an apple,
Just to look at and to hold.

CHANTY

WHEN rain falls, I say
Blow, blow away, sorrow,
It's a foul day today,
But it won't be tomorrow:
Blow away, blow away,
Blow, blow away, sorrow;
It's a foul day today,
But it won't be tomorrow.

As I walked in a glade
Blow, blow away, sorrow,
I met with a maid,
But she won't be tomorrow:
Blow away, blow away,
Blow, blow away, sorrow;
It's a foul day today,
But it won't be tomorrow.

And kiss whom you may,
Blow, blow away, sorrow,
She is yours for today,
But she won't be tomorrow:
Blow away, blow away,
Blow, blow away, sorrow;
It's a foul day today,
But it won't be tomorrow.

So all sing with me
Blow, blow away, sorrow,
And be happy to be,
For we won't be tomorrow:
Blow away, blow away,
Blow, blow away, sorrow;
It's a foul day today,
But it won't be tomorrow.

THE TWO CHRONOMETERS

Two chronometers the captain had,
One by Arnold that ran like mad,
One by Kendal in a walnut case,
Poor devoted creature with a hangdog face.

Arnold always hurried with a crazed click-click
Dancing over Greenwich like a lunatic,
Kendal panted faithfully his watch-dog beat,
Climbing out of Yesterday with sticky little feet.

Arnold choked with appetite to wolf up time,
Madly round the numerals his hands would climb,
His cogs rushed over and his wheels ran miles,
Dragging Captain Cook to the Sandwich Isles.

But Kendal dawdled in the tombstoned past,
With a sentimental prejudice to going fast,
And he thought very often of a haberdasher's door
And a yellow-haired boy who would knock no more.

All through the night-time, clock talked to clock,
In the captain's cabin, tock-tock-tock,
One ticked fast and one ticked slow,
And Time went over them a hundred years ago.

OLD MR TATTERLOCK

OLD Mr Tatterlock walks quite slow;
His joints are stiff and he taps his stick.
I go a-rush and a-tumble-O,
And my racing feet cry: *'Quick, quick, quick'*.

Old Mr Tatterlock's boots are bright.
Just footpath walks are the walks he takes,
With never a speck of mud in sight,
So his toes have stars that the sunlight makes.

I love puddles and gutters and ruts
And the rough red tracks that the wagons choose;
Old Mr Tatterlock tut-tut-tuts
And blinks at the mud on my old brown shoes.

If ever my feet stop flying quick—
I hope they won't but you never can tell—
If my joints grow stiff and I tap my stick
And keep my shoes shone ever so well,

Then I'll meet boys who have been for walks
On the rough red tracks that the wagons choose,
And I'll mimic the way Old Tatterlock talks
And tut-tut-tut at their mud-splashed shoes.

BARGAIN BASEMENT

Not there, my dear, not there:
this way—down the stair.

Have you a line of hillocks and some white
absurd young lambs, all wool, and light
as leaping air?

No, sir—sorry! . . .
Alright, don't worry.

You keep, perhaps
some inexpensive scraps
of early green
springtime sateen,
with colour partly lost
in folds of frost,
prinked with those flowers that smell
so sweetly?—I know them well
but can't recall the name:
I saw them somewhere a month ago.

Unfortunately, madam, no. . . .
Ah, what a shame!

I say, I'd like a length of thin
pale sea-water to wear next to the skin.
None? A creek, then?—with embroideries
of eucalypt trees,
the soldierly sort that gets
dignity from its golden epaulets.

No, sir, impossible. . . .
Oh, well—

Then, do you stock
that delicate sort of frock
now worn by blossoming orchards, thin,
wide and airy, like a crinoline?

No, madam, no; but I might find . . .
O, never mind.

Come on, my dear:
there's nothing for us here.
Thank goodness, we still have, in the Lay By
(for what it's worth
when we two die)
that remnant double-width of damaged earth.

CONQUISTADOR

I SING of the decline of Henry Clay
Who loved a white girl of uncommon size.
Although a small man in a little way,
He had in him some seed of enterprise.

Each day he caught the seven-thirty train
To work, watered his garden after tea,
Took an umbrella if it looked like rain
And was remarkably like you or me.

He had his hair cut once a fortnight, tried
Not to forget the birthday of his wife,
And might have lived unnoticed till he died
Had not ambition entered Henry's life.

He met her in the lounge of an hotel
—A most unusual place for him to go—
But there he was and there she was as well
Sitting alone. He ordered beers for two.

She was so large a girl that when they came
He gave the waiter twice the usual tip.
She smiled without surprise, told him her name
And as the name trembled on Henry's lip

His parched soul, swelling like a desert root,
Broke out its delicate dream upon the air;
The mountains shook with earthquake under foot;
An angel seized him suddenly by the hair;

The sky was shrill with peril as he passed;
A hurricane crushed his senses with its din;
The wildfire crackled up his reeling mast;
The trumpet of a maelstrom sucked him in;

The desert shrivelled and burnt off his feet;
His bones and buttons an enormous snake
Vomited up; still in the shimmering heat
The pygmies showed him their forbidden lake

And then transfixed him with their poison darts;
He married six black virgins in a bunch,
Who, when they had drawn out his manly parts,
Stewed him and ate him lovingly for lunch.

Adventure opened wide its grisly jaws;
Henry looked in and knew the Hero's doom.
The huge white girl drank on without a pause
And, just at closing time, she asked him home.

The tram they took was full of Roaring Boys
Announcing the world's ruin and Judgment Day;
The sky blared with its grand orchestral voice
The Götterdämmerung of Henry Clay.

But in her quiet room they were alone.
There, towering over Henry by a head,
She stood and took her clothes off one by one,
And then she stretched herself upon the bed.

Her bulk of beauty, her stupendous grace
Challenged the lion heart in his puny dust.
Proudly his Moment looked him in the face:
He rose to meet it as a hero must;

Climbed the white mountain of unravished snow,
Planted his tiny flag upon the peak.
The smooth drifts, scarcely breathing, lay below.
She did not take the trouble to smile or speak.

And afterwards, it may have been in play,
The enormous girl rolled over and squashed him flat;
And, as she could not send him home that way,
Used him thereafter as a bedside mat.

Speaking at large, I will say this of her:
She did not spare expense to make him nice.
Tanned on both sides and neatly edged with fur
The job would have been cheap at any price.

And when, in winter, getting out of bed,
Her large soft feet pressed warmly on the skin,
The two glass eyes would sparkle in his head,
The jaws extend their papier-maché grin.

Good people, for the soul of Henry Clay
Offer your prayers, and view his destiny!
He was the Hero of our Time. He may
With any luck, one day, be you or me.

MAD JASPER

MAD Jasper stood poised on the skyscraper wall
and felt this the moment to end all
the desires he'd never get,
to leap from his life's concrete parapet.
He watched the silly dawn arise,
the trams creep up the hollow hill,
the railway's mass of glassy flies
snouting out of the morning's chill.
He had aspired to be in this,
to be the man of the midnight kiss,
the dancing doll of the pubtalk shams,
to pivot straps on the rocking trams.
Yet he'd always been on this lofty sheer,
never tasted the poppysweet,
never flared in the anemone-clear
touch of hands in the moving street.
And now high up in the morning's pall
saw he'd never been down to the street at all.

In anguish mad Jasper loosened his grip
and established one true relationship.

A DRUNKEN MAN ON HIGHGATE HILL:

ALONG the dark wet lanes of golden light
A midnight tippler lurches towards the night.
Bold on earth's edge, against the city's glow, he stands
And signals silence.
        Universes cease
Their clamorous gyrations. All is peace.

Then, with wide-sweeping hands,
He wakes to crashing concord the massed bands
Of all creation; till, reverberate,
Tremble both earth and superstructed dome.
Leading some mad gay march, with pride elate,
Man, drunk with heady power, goes singing home.

Lord of all harmony, he grunts his raucous bars
Where street lamps blaze far brighter than the stars.

FANTASY

I LOVE to lie under the lemon
    That grows by the fountain;
To see the stars flutter and open
    Along the blue mountain.

To hear the last wonderful piping
    That rises to heaven,—
Six quavers to sum up delight in,
    And sorrow in seven—

To dream that the mythic wood-women,
    Each brown as the honey
The bees took their toll of from Hybla,
    On days that were sunny,

Come parting the hedge of my garden
    To dance a light measure
With soft little feet on the greensward,
    Peak-pointed for pleasure.

While Pan, on a leopard reclining,
    And birds on his shoulder,
Gives breath to a flute's wanton sighing
    Until their eyes smoulder.

Then, lo, in the pool of the valley,
    Cries centaur to centaur,
As, plashing, they leap the white moonbuds
    The goddess had leant o'er.

They climb the steep sides of the chasm
    With hollowy thunder—
Whole cliffs at the stroke of their hoof-beats
    Split tumbling asunder!

They climb the steep sides of the chasm,
    And rush through the thicket
That chokes up the pathways that lead to
    My green garden-wicket.

They seize on the dancing wood-women,
   And kick poor Pan over
The back of his fat spotted leopard
   Amid the lush clover.

So I wake, and eagerly listen—
   But only the fountain,
Still sleeping and sobbing, complains at
   The foot of the mountain.

TWELVE O'CLOCK BOAT

ONLY the creaking murmur of the wheel,
The trembling of the engines as they turn;
The ferry glides upon an even keel,
And Pinchgut squats in shadow hard astern. . . .

The lips of ocean murmur at delay.
The lovely moon no longer will refuse,
And from the arms of darkness slips away
To tryst with young Ephesians on Vaucluse,

Naked as when some mercenary Greek
The galleys bore to Carthage stared the sky,
Feeling a wind Sicilian on his cheek,
And fell asleep with no more hope than I

Of life eternal, love, or length of days,
Dreaming he saw his Macedonian home;
Awoke, and duly went his ordered ways
To die at Zama, on the swords of Rome.

But what was moon to him, and what was sea
Two thousand years before myself was born,
Are sickle moon and silver yet to me,
Though Scipio should wait upon Cremorne.

THE MISSAL

THE lovely, lost, italic curve
Enrapt his soul. All day he stared
At A for Apple, dimly heard
The beating of the holy wings
In D for Dove, but shut his ears
To sound's delight, instead preferred
The E of Eden, marked how stood
The mainstroke like a flaming sword.
Then F for Fall—how brief the flight
With dark descender, black as night.
The circumscribed, enchanting sweep
Of G was Goodness. Calm and strong,
Gently it led his eye along
Delicious pastures of the page.
Then, overleaf, before him burned
The winged and serifed letter H
And Heaven was his to have and hold—
Oh missal wrought in holy gold.

The arrogance of earthly power,
Swash capitals for Kings and Men,
Diminished as he turned again
And summoned all his art to raise
The lettered record of his praise—
'Ere there was beast or fish or bird,
Before the Voice of Man was heard,
In the Beginning was the Word.'

THE POSSUM AND THE MOON

I

WHERE a twisted tree
Split the rough sandstone,
I stood at night and heard
A possum scold the moon.

I listened for the cock
Who would call my dead
Grandfather from his grave
To my grandmother's bed.

I waited for the magpie
An hour before the dawn
To sing 'Tan tara, boys!'
On old John Bax's horn.

I lifted up my hand
And made my ear a cup;
The skewbald dingo slept
At Brigalow Gap.

The only sounds I heard
That hour before the light
Were the tide in the leaves,
The possum's cry to the night.

II

I heard the possum cry
Beneath the yellow moon.
I said 'That moon was made
From this same sandstone.'

The moon looked through the trees
And where her shadows stood,
Blackmen sprang upright;
They filled the ancient wood.

A tide ran through the leaves;
Otherwise a still
Hush lay on the bush
Where the shadows fell.

Like a lubra the land
Lay quiet, indifferent.
The shadows stole to the trees
At the moon's ascent.

THE MIMSHI MAIDEN

ROUND the island of Zipangu,
Crowned with lilies, silver-sandal'd,
Through the amber bending bamboo,
In a rickshaw, many-candled,
Rode a tiny Mimshi maiden,
Mimshi, princess of Zipangu,
To the temple where she prayed in . . .
Drums and trumpets! (Such a bang, you
Never heard in all creation—)
Stunned the moonlight! And they sang too,
With one voice, the Mimshi nation!

Through the thickets strolled a yellow
Onyx-taloned, whisker-curling,
Evil-omened tiger-fellow.
Ribs and muscles! Tail up-twirling!
Starved and thirsty, hardly pleasant,
Crouching on his twenty pincers,
Grinned he down o'er lord and peasant,
Baring top and bottom mincers,
Growled, and swore he'd have their princess!
Not a soul but leapt to cover . . .
Priest and boy, two-handed sworder;
All except one rickshaw-shover,
Victim of some queer disorder
Which became a (such his cunning)
Proof of valour, in that he did
Stand his ground, instead of running,
While the bigwigs yet receded:
Worse than any—Mishu-Mishu,
He the princess pledged to marry,
Climbed a loquat, dodged the issue,
Almost scared to *hara-kari*;
Never grew a man so soon white—
Still the tiger did a toe-trot,
Elegantly striped with moonlight,
Round poor Mishu, up his loquat.

Strange that, of the whole procession,
Not a Zoomi pulled an arrow;
Truth to tell, through intercession
June the seventh (signed Ko Tahro,
Mimshi Monarch), every marksman
Had, in honour, as was rightful,
Left his ticklers with a craftsman
Who could make them doubly frightful,
Hence it happened, all the forces
Stood like shadows, inorganic,
Save the buglers, who, on horses,
Spurred to . . . nowhere . . . in a panic.

Gaily pranced the princely tiger,
Past the rickshaw, merely saying
'None so nice or sweet as I . . . Gurr!
Let us two—Gurr! . . . go a-Maying.'

Then he turned him to the coolie;
Stuck him in the rearward haulers,
Showed his teeth, said 'Pully-pully!'
Took the front ones in his maulers . . .

Far away, across Zipangu,
Fled he with the Mimshi maiden
Through the amber bending bamboo
Past the temple where she prayed in,
Past the Forty Singing-Fountains
Where the ring-throats fly in millions,
Golden, from the Golden Mountains,
Through the Seventeen Pavilions.
Thenceforth upward, tracing alleys
Where the dead men, drunk with knowledge,
Stuffed in classes, burst the valleys
With the laughter of their college.
Under falling blooms of Pomo,
Dimly anthered, like the moon,
Eyed like women dear old Homer,
Child of Smyrna, sang the rune,
Came the tiger to the river—
Stones across the splashing water

Took him safely, without quiver,
Took him—and Ko Tahro's daughter,
While he whispered 'I can kiss you
. Ninety kisses to the minute;
You won't miss your Mishu-Mishu—
Mishu-Mishu isn't in it.'

Mimshi felt she must adore him,
(Such things sometimes do grow fixtures),
Loved the tiger; and she bore him
Little Mimshi-tiger mixtures.

THE RETREAT FROM HEAVEN

THE armies joined; I saw the Prince of Peace
Desert his Staff of twelve, and then advance,
Beneath the swirling snow that would not cease,
To greet the waiting Emperor of France.

The soldiers laughed, unloosing belt and pack;
Now was the fighting done, the end in sight.
For comrades left to wolves along the track
They sighed, who'd rest in Heaven's beds that night.

The leaders now agreed upon their plan,
And to the Gates of Heaven turned their feet.
First to regain the citadel of man,
Their footsteps echoed down the hollow street.

All was deserted; walls gave back the sound
Of nothing but their voices, rising shrill
In wonderment at this, the holy ground,
This skeleton of cities, frozen still.

Bare were the windows, and the doors were wide,
The rooms were empty as a stranded shell.
Each drew the other closer to his side. . . .
Deep in the soundless city clanged a bell.

Napoleon shivered; blanched was Jesus' cheek,
And coldly glistened sweat upon each brow;
Dry lips refused, but eyes remained, to speak
The question voiceless: Master, whither now?

Napoleon turned, and Jesus called his name;
They paused, and then fled headlong down the street. . . .
The waiting armies marked a distant flame,
Then heard the bugles sounding the retreat.

They saw their leaders' carriage thunder past,
And Rumour whispered, until Panic cried;
A musket cracked; defiant, scornful, last
Stood Michel Ney, with Peter at his side.

THE NICORN'S DOWER

ONLY the nicorn knows
what hides beyond the hills
only the crownéd snow-white haunter
of snow-hushed rills,
that fumbles with eager lips
at the tingling breast of the snow
(and his hooves tattooing the frozen
spine of the sleeper
who wakes to the golden echoes
and shakes and thrills);
only he and the stag
and the high-questing ounce
and the vikingly-pinioned crag-keeper
hung high o'er the source
whence the uttermost cataract spills—
these span the divide
and they know
the paths where the wild sheep go
to the tracts where the strange winds course
that swoop on us down from the hills
like atomy porcupine-quills
elf-volleyed from turrets of snow.

THE ORANGE TREE

THE young girl stood beside me. I
  Saw not what her young eyes could see:
—A light, she said, not of the sky
  Lives somewhere in the Orange Tree.

—Is it, I said, of east or west?
  The heartbeat of a luminous boy
Who with his faltering flute confessed
  Only the edges of his joy?

Was he, I said, borne to the blue
  In a mad escapade of Spring
Ere he could make a fond adieu
  To his love in the blossoming?

—Listen! the young girl said. There calls
  No voice, no music beats on me;
But it is almost sound: it falls
  This evening on the Orange Tree.

—Does he, I said, so fear the Spring
  Ere the white sap too far can climb?
See in the full gold evening
  All happenings of the olden time?

Is he so goaded by the green?
  Does the compulsion of the dew
Make him unknowable but keen
  Asking with beauty of the blue?

—Listen! the young girl said. For all
  Your hapless talk you fail to see
There is a light, a step, a call,
  This evening on the Orange Tree.

—Is it, I said, a waste of love
  Imperishably old in pain,
Moving as an affrighted dove
  Under the sunlight or the rain?

Is it a fluttering heart that gave
    Too willingly and was reviled?
Is it the stammering at a grave,
    The last word of a little child?

—Silence! the young girl said. Oh, why,
    Why will you talk to weary me?
Plague me no longer now, for I
    Am listening like the Orange Tree.

FINE CLAY

O WHITE clay, O fine clay of the earth cold,
  Him I fashion cunningly surely will be sweet.
Godlike am I moulding him in the god's mould,
  Hands, lips, feet.

Him I fashion delicate surely is more dear
  Than all the strength of Heaven, strength of
    night and day,
More than all the mirrored stars in pools still and clear,
  Him that I am fashioning of fine white clay.

Him I fashion cunningly surely will be fair.
  Oh the fine white clay that in the earth lies!
As the gods I fashion him, lips, hands, hair,
  Hands, lips, eyes.

Ah, alas, I wonder, now that Evening's shade
  Like a purple shadow on earth's grass is spread,
Will the gods love him, made as they are made,
  Hands, lips, head?

Ah, shall they, the flower-crowned gods, whose eyes
    are bright,
  Take him as their play-thing to break in their play?
More is he than all the gods who watch day and night,
  Him that I am fashioning of fine white clay.

THE EVENING GLEAM

THE evening gleam of still waters
Can stay the feet that roam,
As if the soul in its long homelessness
Came suddenly home.

I know not still what beauty is.
I would ask the wise:
What verity is half discovered here
For too dim eyes?

Something of otherworldly kind,
More than the thing seen;
Something possessed a moment, other
Than light and form mean.

Beauty is simple and austere.
Is it all of sense and time?
The evening gleam of still waters
Mocks art of rhyme.

H

BEAUTY OF THE WORLD

Not what men see,
Not what they draw from the spread
Of hills looming in cloud—
Not this makes them proud;
But what they can hold in fee
With difficulty and dread
To tell to their hearts in pain
Over and over again.

The terror of Beauty is this:
That something may find the abyss,
Some fact of miracle that you have seen
And no one ever know it ever has been
Nor what its miracle would mean.

The spacious suns
Flow through the heart as water runs,
Known and not held,
Leaving no trace.
O'er Earth's wind-ruffled face
Goes the sun-shuddering air. . . .
Of all the Beauty that rides
Violent or velvet-footed everywhere,
So little abides—
The hunger of life's unquelled!
So rarely, rarely can these vistas draw
Deep in the spirit their trails of speechless awe!

Languid upon their slopes of silvery death
Dead giants sway to the noon breezes' breath;
How these things torture the soul!
Moonlight that loiters on a mossy bole;
Sunglow that makes a pillow of a stone;
The drifts of forest light;
Trees in a stormy night;
Bush echoes; ocean's unresolving tone,
Or groups of falling chords melting to one;
The softness of a kookaburra's crown
The breeze puts softly up and softly down;
His eyes of love that almost humanly speak
Peering in softness o'er that murderous beak!

Gardens will blossom forever, breaking the spirit,
All your endeavour be guerdonless, trammelled
    with dross;
Vain the accomplishing ardours the races inherit
Till true men open their mouths, confessing
    their loss.
Beauty strides like a warrior, tortures the passions,
Troubles the soul with its mountainous loveliness;
Vain what we yearn toward, vain all the deft
    hand fashions
Till, turning toward the ranges, men confess
That they shall trouble overmuch
For things they'll never touch,
That forests they move among
Shall always elude their yearning
And all their passion be as the returning
Silence when the thrush has sung.

When, folded on gully and crown,
The west light spreads the shadows down
And daylight dies on unapproachable hills,
The breathing silence storms us, the heart fills,
We're sated with sublimity. . . .
But, having tramped those tracks and crossed
    those rills
Nearing their slopes, the mountains cease to be.

Full well we know
Must pass, must pass away
This joy, that woe;
And learn full well in quiet dismay
That Beauty cannot stay.
But this content for which we vainly grope,
This desperate reach for miracle may give place
By an intenser waiting, a more passionate hope,
To nobleness in small things, acts of grace.

BEAUTY AND TERROR

BEAUTY does not walk through lovely days,
Beauty walks with horror in her hair;
Down long centuries of pleasant ways
Men have found the terrible most fair.

Youth is lovelier in death than life,
Beauty mightier in pain than joy,
Doubly splendid burn the fires of strife
Brighter than the brightness they destroy.

I HAVE GOLDEN SHOES

I HAVE golden shoes
To make me fleet,
They are like the wind
Underneath my feet.

When my lover's kiss
Is overbold,
I can run away
In my shoes of gold.

Nay, when I am shod
With this bright fire,
I am forced to run
From my own desire.

From the love I love
Whose arms enfold
I must run away
In my shoes of gold.

SONG FOR LOVERS

LOVE needs no pondered words,
  No high philosophy;
Enough the singing birds
  In the green tree.

Enough the touch of hand,
  Whose trembling worship tells
Faiths deeper than command
  Cathedral bells.

Blood sings fresh truths that wise
  Old Plato never knew;
Dimmed are thought's evening eyes
  By sun on dew.

Come rainbow or the rose,
  Vision shall find new birth:
With love more lovely grows
  Beauty on earth.

Darkly death waits, yet we
  In a wild hour shall know
Bright immortality,
  Before we go.

LOVE'S COMING

QUIETLY as rosebuds
   Talk to the thin air,
Love came so lightly
   I knew not he was there.

Quietly as lovers
   Creep at the middle moon,
Softly as players tremble
   In the tears of a tune;

Quietly as lilies
   Their faint vows declare
Came the shy pilgrim:
   I knew not he was there.

Quietly as tears fall
   On a wild sin,
Softly as griefs call
   In a violin;

Without hail or tempest,
   Blue sword or flame,
Love came so lightly
   I knew not that he came.

SHE LIKE THE MOON ARISES

SHE like the moon arises
And tranquil sees beyond dark window-bars
The exquisite circumspection of the stars
Treading the heavenly floor.

And insolent hope surprises
My sole heart that darkness held in pawn
And sheds the spurious glimmer of a dawn
Upon the infinite, the nevermore.

IN A CONVEX MIRROR

SEE, in the circle how we stand,
As pictured angels touching wings
Inflame a Dutch interior
Bespeaking birth, foretelling kings.

The room is still and brushed with dusk;
Shall we not disregard the clock
Or let alone be eloquent
The silence between tick and tock?

Shall we be fixed within the frame,
This breathing light to clear-cold glass
Until our images are selves
And words to wiser silence pass?

But ruined Rostov falls in flame,
Cities crumble and are gone,
Time's still waters deeply flow
Through Here and Now as Babylon.

And swirling through this little frame
Will rive the two of us apart,
Engulfing with unnumbered floods
The hidden spaces of the heart.

CELEBRATION OF LOVE

ALL things announce her coming and her praise:
The evening sun, awake in bright dry air;
The invisible patterns of the wind, that fade
To stillness and then faintly reappear,
Alternate as my hope; the gradual shade
That moves across the lucerne-flats; the sheer
Cloud-shapes, leaning on the stony sill
Of distant ranges folded in blue haze;
The river, gliding smoothly as my will
Beneath the solitary heron's gaze;
The trees upon the hill: the living day's
External presences attend and bless
Her coming with an inward happiness.

Wild creatures to our meeting-hour respond
With new alacrity: the sudden flocks
Of parrots hanging in the summer trees
Scatter with loud cries; shy wallabies
Peer out like secret selves among the rocks;
A clod of earth moves, and becomes a rabbit,
Which races madly round the pond
That glottal frogs inhabit;
Magpies fly up from the grass, and even
Those sober citizens of Sweet Content,
Koalas, feel the tug of the event
And look down from their sleepy galleries
In grave astonishment.

Chance, as if in fear that we may lose
The tensions that invigorate our love,
Draws us continually apart, to prove
That by our distant and opposing motions
The many-stranded cord is twisted stronger.
We were not separate, touching no longer,
Nor lonely, though alone:
Until we made life new I had not known
What force lies in our being to defeat
The emptiness that seems an active power
Assimilating life. But we have grown

So full of being that we can complete
The gap in things where time and fear devour.

Now from her eastern road the moon sets sail
To voyage on the summer map of stars
Between Canopus and the Whale.
Let that celestial mood prevail
In us, that we may set our course
For new discovery, and find the source
Of gleaming intimations that have come
Like meteors from elysium,
As driftwood once foretold American shores.
The continent that we infer
Awaits a bold devout discoverer
And why not we,
Who fear no shipwreck and no mutiny?

Cosmography is infinite for love:
The contours change at every step we move.
Always the eager spirit can explore
Beyond the Wallace line of known delight
To an unmapped premonitory shore.
Our meeting makes this summer night
A new world, with new species, and new dangers;
And we are made new in each other's sight.
For by continual growth love keeps us strangers,
Despite the recognitions that descend
From sense into the soul, and there
Are stored against famine, exile, and despair.

Jupiter himself had no such scope
As man, when his inconstant passions range.
For seven days I could be
Married to a mountain or a tree,
In love with swan, or cat, or antelope;
No love of man is strange.
Besides which, it emerges from the deep
Anterior caverns where it raged, before
It found one chosen object to adore.
How is it then that you can keep
All of my lust contained, unless you be
Akin to bird, beast, mountain, tree,
Of wide creation an epitome?

Yet you are more, being yourself; not merely
A script of symbols where my heart can read
Secrets of its nature and its need
And know itself more clearly.
You are yourself; and when we touch
We understand the joy of being two,
Not seeking to annihilate
Distinction, as self-lovers do. The soul
Is born a solitary; others come
With foreign gestures to it, which it must
Learn patiently by heart, or be unjust.
The god has been a child since men began
To worship him; he must become a man.

Imperfect in imperfect, love
Grows within music. Worlds rejoice
To find their lost identities restored
To morning brightness by a clear voice
Recovering the creative word.
Now with uplifted heart, at light's increase,
I praise in you the stars and waterfalls,
The slow ascent of trees, swiftness of birds,
The innocence and order, the wild calls:
The glowing Ithacan web of faithful earth
Coming to luminous rebirth
In the configurations that belong
To silence, when, dark years of waiting by,
Her gaze is lighted by futurity
And all her secret fountains flow in song.

And touched by sunlight, my words change back
Into the daily acts of life.
—Song, you are too late by many years
To be the epithalamion
That I have owed her; say in my excuse
You are the best of many songs begun.
Fear not to be looked at in the sun,
Your meaning is too plain to be discerned;
And few of those that read you will have learned
That every living fruit the soul can bear
Is born of patience and despair.
Heed none of them; your praises lie elsewhere,
And are not given, but are truly earned.

ENVY GOES GROPING

ENVY goes groping for the kisses
others have had of your mouth's red;
gropes in morass, and thereby misses
these, flowerlike, which have sprung instead—

these which are ageless and not vexed
by ancient jealousy, old grime,
but span this instant and the next,
trembling upon the edge of time,

hawks hung in the wind above that verge
where all falls bottomless and is nought,
whence the tomorrows shall emerge
which yet are cloudy and unwrought.

Poised at time's focus on strong wings,
like birds turned sharply into the gust,
your kisses have linked me to wise things
saner than envy or distrust:

Space for this moment is not more
than a swollen raindrop, which could burst
here at my lips and spill its store
of riches on my clamouring thirst;

and Now, holding its breath, reveals
how each new summer like saved wine
treasures old summers, and conceals
springs yet ungathered, and all mine.

So when I clasp you here I keep
all that dead lovers have desired,
waken their bodies from long sleep
and their dreams, changeless and untired.

Held thus, you become drawn breath of any
who have been loved—once named, once known;
and the brief lives of that white many
you hand on, deathless and your own.

There is only this embrace at last
anywhere: others touched you once,
but I touch all the present and past
and the wide sky's uncounted suns.

THE COMPANY OF LOVERS

WE meet and part now over all the world,
we, the lost company,
take hands together in the night, forget
the night in our brief happiness, silently.
We who sought many things, throw all away
for this one thing, one only,
remembering that in the narrow grave
we shall be lonely.

Death marshals up his armies round us now.
Their footsteps crowd too near.
Lock your warm hand above the chilling heart
and for a time I live without my fear.
Grope in the night to find me and embrace,
for the dark preludes of the drums begin,
and round us, round the company of lovers,
Death draws his cordons in.

THERE SLEEPS IN THE CHURCHYARD

THERE sleeps in the churchyard who might say,
'I'm through with the toys that fill your day.
You may spend my money, and seethe my hog,
And scatter the bones of my faithful dog,
When you lime my fields to grow your grain:
And little you'll profit and nothing gain,
For you'll come to the end that I knew, at length,
For all your striving and all your strength.'
  And, walking here, neath the hot, quick sky,
  'I'm one with you there, my friend,' say I.
  'You may draw these down 'neath your mound so still,
  For all I account of them, good or ill.
  You can reckon me out of your testament
  Of aught that was borrowed or thieved or lent
  When you walked, as I walk, under the sky:
  And much may they profit the dead, say I!'

There sleeps in the churchyard who might say,
'I'm quit of the loves that warmed my day.
You may wed my widow, or seek a maid,
The spit of a score with whom I played.
You may get you issue within the law,
Or catchcolts got in the wild-oat straw:
For you'll come to a lone, cold bed, at last,
For all your loosing or clipping fast.'
  And, gazing down at his mound so green,
  To one who was as myself had been
  Or ever I cried with a passionate cry,
  Nor cried in vain, I make reply,
  'Fade, friend, hasten and fade away!
  Fade murmur to Murmuring, clay to Clay!
  Fade cold to Cold and rime to Rime!
  Fade quag to Quag in the Slough of Time!

'But know, ere thine ear be drained of sound
And thy numbness one with thy stilly mound,
That they who have known one kiss of Love
May lag no more in a six-foot groove,
Nor drowse them adown into death's frore fire

That crumbles the cinders of all desire;
But ever they circle and wheel and cry
With the wind that bells in the crystal sky:
  In the cry of the bird and the cry of the heart,
  Thenceforth and forever these have their part;
  And theirs is the voice that is never still
  Whose yearning is flung from hill to hill,
  From mountain to mountain and deep to deep,
  Through the whorls of waking and coils of sleep;
  Nor peace shall come to them ever again,
  Though Midir return for his lost Etaine.
For the wind that blows and the wind that bells
Is wound and bound by the oldest spells
That bind but to loose and to bind again
Into a hell-spite hurricane
That whirls from the Branch of the Hazel Tree
The bound and helpless atomy,
That the earth may nourish a new Etaine
To mortals' schooling and mortals' pain.'

THE KNIFE

WHEN shall I expel you from my blood?
When drive you forth from the heart of me,
Untwist you from my nerves, tear you forcibly
Free from my brain? O if I could

Sever you from the pulse that beats all day
Far in the deep, labyrinthine soul of me,
Cut you from my sinews, and deliberately
Rise and thrust you once for all away.

Except a lancet bid it silence keep
How shall I still my tongue from calling you?
How shall I stay my hands from holding you—
When they stretch out to find you even in sleep?

The wind shall sooner wear away the stone
Than I obliterate you from the bone.

J

COUNTRY DANCE

THE dance in the township hall is nearly over.
Hours ago the stiff-handed wood-cheeked women
got up from the benches round the walls
and took home their aching eyes and weary children.
Mrs McLarty with twenty cows to milk
before dawn, went with the music stinging
like sixty wasps under her best dress.
Eva Callaghan whose boy died in the army
sat under the streamers like a house to let
and went alone, a black pot brimming with tears.
'Once my body was a white cedar, my breasts the buds
        on the quince-tree,
that now are fallen and grey like logs on a cleared hill.
Then why is my blood not quiet? what is the good
of the whips of music stinging along my blood?'

The dance in the township hall is nearly over.
Outside in the yard the fire like a great red city
eats back into the log, its noisy flames fallen.
Jimmy Dunn has forgotten his camp in the hills
and sleeps like a heap of rags beside a bottle.
The young boys sit and stare at the heart of the city
thinking of the neon lights and the girls at the corners
with lips like coals and thighs as silver as florins.
Jock Hamilton thinks of the bally cow gone sick
and the cockatoos in the corn and the corn ready to pick
and the wires in the thirty-acre broken.
Oh, what rats nibble at the cords of our nerves?
When will the wires break, the ploughed paddocks lie
        open,
the bow of the fiddle saw through the breast-bone,
the dream be done, and we waken?

Streamers and boughs are falling, the dance grows faster.
Only the lovers and the young are dancing
now at the end of a dance, in a trance or singing.
Say the lovers locked together and crowned with coloured
        paper,

'The bit of black glass I picked up out of the campfire
is the light the moon puts on your hair.'
'The green pool I swam in under the willows
is the drowning depth, the summer night of your eyes.'
'You are the death I move to.' 'O burning weapon,
you are the pain I long for.'

Stars, leaves and streamers fall in the dark dust
and the blind man lies alone in his sphere of night.

Oh, I,
red centre of a dark and burning sky,
fit my words to music, my crippled words to music,
and sing to the fire with the voice of the fire.
Go sleep with your grief, go sleep with your desire,
go deep into the core of night and silence.
But I hold all of it, your hate and sorrow,
your passion and your fear; I am the breath
that holds you from your death.
I am the voice of music and the ended dance.

YOU'LL KNOW LOVE

Love's a hussy when you know her;
She hardly waits the chance to show her
Charms to every sort of people.
Love's a sky for any steeple.

Life, when first I heard about it,
Left no room for me to doubt it:
This gay passion seemed as simple
As the softness of a dimple.

Orange-blossoms hide the urchin
Wearing silks to go to church in,
Watched by window-saints the colour
Of her blushes, only duller.

Often, solemn persons slowly
Outline love or prove it holy;
Listen so as not to grieve them;
Nod your head—but don't believe them.

Don't believe them: no one ever
Learnt by being good or clever.
You'll know love when it has taken
Body and soul and left both shaken.

LOVE ME AND NEVER LEAVE ME

Love me, and never leave me,
Love, nor ever deceive me,
And I shall always bless you
If I may undress you:
  Which I heard a lover say
  To his sweetheart where they lay.

He, though he did undress her,
Did not always bless her;
She, though she would not leave him,
Often did deceive him;
  Yet they loved, and when they died
  They were buried side by side.

THE PASSIONATE CLERK TO HIS LOVE

LIVE with me; be my wife;
  We'll end flirtations;
You'll find it a slow life,
  But with compensations.

And we'll get a flat
  Of two witty
Rooms, a bath and kitchenette,
  High over the city,

Where, in the evening
  When dinner's over,
We'll wash up everything
  And I'll be your lover,

And tie knot after knot
  Of flesh aching,
Then cut the lot,
  And without waking

You'll sleep till sunrise,
  And we'll rise early,
And through each other's eyes
  We'll see things clearly,

And never be dismayed
  To find them shoddy,
And never be afraid
  Of anybody;

And on Sunday afternoon
  About three or four
I'll play the gramophone
  While you pour

Afternoon tea
  Into my soul,
And bending to me
  With the sugar bowl

You'll be a priestess
  Swaying the sheathing
Of a flower-stained dress
  With even breathing

And in this atmosphere
  Charmed from your breast
Half we shall hear
  And feel the rest

As we talk scandal and
  A kind of wit
We alone understand,
  Or maybe just sit

Quiet while the clock chimes
  Patient tomorrows,
And smile sometimes
  At old sorrows.

SONG OF THE RAIN

NIGHT,
And the yellow pleasure of candle-light . . .
Old brown books and the kind fine face of the clock
Fogged in the veils of the fire—its cuddling tock.

The cat,
Greening her eyes on the flame-litten mat;
Wickedly wakeful she yawns at the rain
Bending the roses over the pane,
And a bird in my heart begins to sing
Over and over the same sweet thing—

'Safe in the house with my boyhood's love,
And our children asleep in the attic above.'

LOVE IN AGE

WHERE the fountain murmurs in the shade
Gilds the leaning lily stems with dew
Lovelier than the mystery of birth,

Stars the drooping iris hearts with light
Brighter than the radiances of life,
Two old lovers speak of love in age.

'Gone are the days when as you lay beside me
Your foot with tender intent
Touched mine, my love, or your knee or shoulder
tried me
As you leant
To find my lips, content.

'Gone are the days. How would you now deride me
Should service of Eve augment
My love, or I with lure or blandishment provide me
When you bent
To touch my lips content.'

Still, the fountain, murmurous in shade;
Still, the leaning lilies, wet with dew;
Gone the lovers to a longer night.

HOUSE-MATES

Because his soup was cold, he needs must sulk
From dusk till dark, and never speak to her;
And all the time she heard his heavy bulk
Blunder about the house, making a stir
In this room and in that. She heard him mutter
His foolish breathless noises, snarling and thick.
She knew the very words he first would utter;
He always said them, and they made her sick—
Those awkward efforts at a gracious peace
And kindly patronage of high-forgiving.
She knew these quarrelling calms would never cease
As long as she could keep his body living;
And so she lay and felt the hours creep by,
Wondering lazily upon her bed,
How cold the world would be if he should die
And leave her weeping for her stupid dead.

EVE-SONG

I SPAN and Eve span
A thread to bind the heart of man;
But the heart of man was a wandering thing
That came and went with little to bring:
Nothing he minded what we made,
As here he loitered, and there he stayed.

I span and Eve span
A thread to bind the heart of man;
But the more we span the more we found
It wasn't his heart but ours we bound.
For children gathered about our knees:
The thread was a chain that stole our ease.
And one of us learned in our children's eyes
That more than man was love and prize.
But deep in the heart of one of us lay
A root of loss and hidden dismay.

He said he was strong. He had no strength
But that which comes of breadth and length.
He said he was fond. But his fondness proved
The flame of an hour when he was moved.
He said he was true. His truth was but
A door that winds could open and shut.

And yet, and yet, as he came back,
Wandering in from the outward track,
We held our arms, and gave him our breast,
As a pillowing place for his head to rest.
I span and Eve span,
A thread to bind the heart of man!

WOMAN TO MAN

THE eyeless labourer in the night,
the selfless, shapeless seed I hold,
builds for its resurrection day—
silent and swift and deep from sight
foresees the unimagined light.

This is no child with a child's face;
this has no name to name it by:
yet you and I have known it well.
This is our hunter and our chase,
the third who lay in our embrace.

This is the strength that your arm knows,
the arc of flesh that is my breast,
the precise crystals of our eyes.
This is the blood's wild tree that grows
the intricate and folded rose.

This is the maker and the made;
this is the question and reply;
the blind head butting at the dark,
the blaze of light along the blade.
Oh hold me, for I am afraid.

THE UNBORN

I

I KNOW no sleep you do not stand beside.
You footless darkness following where I go,
you lipless drinker at my drowsy breast—
yet whom I must deny I have denied.
The unpossessing is the unpossessed.

Slight is the foothold from the well of night,
the stair is broken and the keys are lost,
and you whom I have wrecked are wrecked indeed;
and yet you stand upon the edge of sight,
and I have known no path you have not crossed.

The shadow wakeful on my sleeping arm
stares from the hidden depths far under birth.
How like a diamond looks the far-off day,
that crystal that reflects your darkened dream,
that bubble of sunlight broken and blown away.
O gift ungiven. O uncreated earth.

II

Not even tears were mine,
not even death;
not even the dazzling pain
of one first breath.

I never knew the sleep
of the warm womb.
The end of my beginning
was dumb; was dumb.

Only the foot of the stair
I felt, being blind.
Then came the touch of fear
time now can never mend.

My name was a dark sound
that made no word.
Terror alone spoke it
and nothing heard.

Neither awake nor asleep
on the rack of dark I lie,
hearing my own not-voice,
'What was I? I? I?'

DEATH IS BUT DEATH

THERE is no soft beatitude in Death:
  Death is but Death;
  Nor can I find
  Him pale and kind
Who set that endless silence on her breath.
  Death is but Death!

There is no hidden comeliness in grief:
  Grief is but Grief;
  Nor for thy ill
  Canst thou distil
An unguent from the laurel's bitter leaf.
  Grief is but Grief!

There is no potent anodyne in tears:
  Tears are but Tears;
  Nor can the woe
  Of green wounds grow
Less green for their salt kindness through the years.
  Tears are but Tears!

PLANET MOON

PLANET moon and dancing star
Round my mother's forehead are
Like a dust of golden bees
Droning in the honey trees.

But oh! the sadness of her face
Was a twilight in God's place—
And her eyes with weeping made
Mists along His lovely glade. . . .

FIVE BELLS

Time that is moved by little fidget wheels
Is not my Time, the flood that does not flow.
Between the double and the single bell
Of a ship's hour, between a round of bells
From the dark warship riding there below,
I have lived many lives, and this one life
Of Joe, long dead, who lives between five bells.

Deep and dissolving verticals of light
Ferry the falls of moonshine down. Five bells
Coldly rung out in a machine's voice. Night and water
Pour to one rip of darkness, the Harbour floats
In air, the Cross hangs upside-down in water.

Why do I think of you, dead man, why thieve
These profitless lodgings from the flukes of thought
Anchored in Time? You have gone from earth,
Gone even from the meaning of a name;
Yet something's there, yet something forms its lips
And hits and cries against the ports of space,
Beating their sides to make its fury heard.

Are you shouting at me, dead man, squeezing your face
In agonies of speech on speechless panes?
Cry louder, beat the windows, bawl your name!

But I hear nothing, nothing . . . only bells,
Five bells, the bumpkin calculus of Time.
Your echoes die, your voice is dowsed by Life,
There's not a mouth can fly the pygmy strait—
Nothing except the memory of some bones
Long shoved away, and sucked away, in mud;
And unimportant things you might have done,
Or once I thought you did; but you forgot,
And all have now forgotten—looks and words
And slops of beer; your coat with buttons off,
Your gaunt chin and pricked eye, and raging tales
Of Irish kings and English perfidy,
And dirtier perfidy of publicans
Groaning to God from Darlinghurst.
                              Five bells.

Then I saw the road, I heard the thunder
Tumble, and felt the talons of the rain
The night we came to Moorebank in slab-dark,
So dark you bore no body, had no face,
But a sheer voice that rattled out of air
(As now you'd cry if I could break the glass),
A voice that spoke beside me in the bush,
Loud for a breath or bitten off by wind,
Of Milton, melons and the Rights of Man,
And blowing flutes, and how Tahitian girls
Are brown and angry-tongued, and Sydney girls
Are white and angry-tongued, or so you'd found.
But all I heard was words that didn't join,
So Milton became melons, melons girls,
And fifty mouths, it seemed, were out that night,
And in each tree an Ear was bending down,
Or something had just run, gone behind grass,
When, blank and bone-white, like a maniac's thought,
The naphtha-flash of lightning slit the sky,
Knifing the dark with deathly photographs.
There's not so many with so poor a purse
Or fierce a need, must fare by night like that,
Five miles in darkness on a country track,
But when you do, that's what you think.
                                         Five bells.

In Melbourne, your appetite had gone,
Your angers too; they had been leeched away
By the soft archery of summer rains
And the sponge-paws of wetness, the slow damp
That stuck the leaves of living, snailed the mind,
And showed your bones, that had been sharp with rage,
The sodden ecstasies of rectitude.
I thought of what you'd written in faint ink,
Your journal with the sawn-off lock, that stayed behind
With other things you left, all without use,
All without meaning now, except a sign
That someone had been living who now was dead:
'At Labassa. Room 6 x 8
On top of the tower; because of this, very dark
And cold in winter. Everything has been stowed
Into this room—500 books all shapes

And colours, dealt across the floor
And over sills and on the laps of chairs;
Guns, photoes of many differant things
And differant curioes that I obtained. . . .'

In Sydney, by the spent aquarium-flare
Of penny gaslight on pink wallpaper,
We argued about blowing up the world,
But you were living backward, so each night
You crept a moment closer to the breast,
And they were living, all of them, those frames
And shapes of flesh that had perplexed your youth,
And most your father, the old man gone blind,
With fingers always round a fiddle's neck,
That graveyard mason whose fair monuments
And tablets cut with dreams of piety
Rest on the bosoms of a thousand men
Staked bone by bone, in quiet astonishment
At cargoes they had never thought to bear,
These funeral-cakes of sweet and sculptured stone.

Where have you gone? The tide is over you,
The turn of midnight water's over you,
As Time is over you, and mystery,
And memory, the flood that does not flow.
You have no suburb, like those easier dead
In private berths of dissolution laid—
The tide goes over, the waves ride over you
And let their shadows down like shining hair,
But they are Water; and the sea-pinks bend
Like lilies in your teeth, but they are Weed;
And you are only part of an Idea.
I felt the wet push its black thumb-balls in,
The night you died, I felt your eardrums crack,
And the short agony, the longer dream,
The Nothing that was neither long nor short;
But I was bound, and could not go that way,
But I was blind, and could not feel your hand.
If I could find an answer, could only find
Your meaning, or could say why you were here
Who now are gone, what purpose gave you breath
Or seized it back, might I not hear your voice?

I looked out of my window in the dark
At waves with diamond quills and combs of light
That arched their mackerel-backs and smacked the sand
In the moon's drench, that straight enormous glaze,
And ships far off asleep, and Harbour-buoys
Tossing their fireballs wearily each to each,
And tried to hear your voice, but all I heard
Was a boat's whistle, and the scraping squeal
Of seabirds' voices far away, and bells,
Five bells. Five bells coldly ringing out.
                                    Five bells.

THE FISHERS

Two men stood thigh-deep in the sea,
Their bodies braced against the pounding surf,
Hauling a net of fishes;
Heel-deep in shifting sand, inch by inch the fishers neared the
    shore,
For heavy was the brown net with sea and fishes,
And the pushing of a great sea-wind against them,
But already gleamed the silver sequins of creatures of the sea,
Their round eyes goggling, and mouths agape for breath.

The two men leant against the wall of wind,
Calm in the sureness of their plunder,
And one, the taller by a head, cried: 'John,
The net is heavy with big fishes',
And laughed and hummed a chanty.

But the man John did not hear, for the wind had him,
Whispering the lisp of his dead love of the spring,
The wind whipped him, but the fires of his heart were drowned,
And the fisher John fished not for fishes,
Nor braced his thighs against the piling sea,
But loosed his tug and let the net go slack,
And the other cried: 'John, the net is loose',
And urged him stiffen 'gainst the fish escape.

The man John heard the voice as one hears shells
Murmuring of things long gone—
Irredeemable springs, and love's laughter dead,
And John the fisher let his net-hold go,
And a great surf took his feet, and tangled them,
Wrapping him to his thighs in twisted flax,
And drew him down,
And sucked him to the deeps.
The net unbent its brown salt length,
And heavy of its trove of man and fishes,
Came shorewards inch by inch to ankle shallows.

While John the fisher lay so still upon the sands,
The fishes quivered, then blindly stared;
So stared the man John—at some far nothingness,
Where the fishes' breath slept, and his one spring song.

ELEGY

HERE, awaiting what hereafter,
Lie lissom love and lyric laughter.

She was born for earth's delight,
Not to couch in earthy night.
Crime against mankind to slay her!
Double crime to rot and clay her!

Let the lord of heaven taste
Bitterly this tragic waste,
See the beauty here destroyed,
View that breast and head left void
Of all that gave their piercing charm,
And weep irreparable harm.

Here, expecting no hereafter,
Lie lissom love and lyric laughter.

LULLABY

GIRL with eyes like dying flowers,
come near and close them and shut out
the elegant spring. You have lived hours
on the moon's lips among night flowers.

If your hand is cold and wet
and your thoughts a cruel cage
let your body stretch to me and set
its marble like disaster in my flesh.

Now your golden hair lies dead
and your arms, so white and brown.
The thorn and the storm your eyes have shed
and they are in me and you are dead.

ENIGMA

I WATCH her fingers while they prance
Like little naked women, tango-mad,
Along the keys, a cup-shot dance—
Music, who'll say, more joyous or more sad?

A mystery . . . but not so strange
As she, Enigma is her pretty name;
And, though she smiles, her veiled eyes range
Through tears of melancholy and shame.

She laughs and weeps . . . Is it because
Only to-night she gave herself to me?
The new bud frightened to be glad . . .
The child's first vision of the insatiate sea.

DRUIDIC GUMS

WHAT padded feet rustle the dead leaves?
What bulking shapes, eyeless, crouch in the gloom
To make the menace of awaiting night?
I am afraid, hemmed in by atavistic gum-trees,
Barbaric, twisted eccentric by demon stresses,
Strange southern acolytes of the eternal Pan.
See! They clench hands of the topmost leaf-clumps,
Thrusting, from thin wrist-boughs, defiance at the sky.
Will they turn at last from throttling the red Scorpion,
Grope downwards, close, and clutch me by the throat?
No grey stones glimmer for ancient altar,
Yet grown druidic the hill's tree-ringed circle,
Dreaming of death-dancing priests, hymns, and whetted
    knives,
Calling for sacrifice, crying for blood!

. . . I have forgotten the terror of druidic gums
With your coming, and the clinging of lips.
You are the night's Bacchante, drinking
Fire from darkness, filling the body with flame . . .
Yet still you strain to keep your self apart,
Thrusting defiance against our imminent heaven
Like the gums' clenched hands, lifted in vain
Against the moving brightness of the stars.

In this unequal strife the hot blood
Campaigns enfoldment; lips make quick marches
On lips, hair, and bended nape.
In this, the electric storm of desire,
Each vein shakes to the pulse thundering,
Echoes rolling, and the forked lightning
Flashes, leaps through the loins—the storm breaks,
And joy, exultant, gushing, sweeps down
From the heavens triumphant, till we, entwining
On the earth, crushing the ferny bracken—
Above us the pointed tongues of gum-leaves touching,
Beside us straight columns of the great gums rising—
Know sweet coolness after rain, peace fragrant
As the dim air around us, eucalyptus-drenched.

Two mopokes, deep-voiced, in the blackness call
From hill to gully, answering, recurring
In liquid music for this melting hour,
Brimming the silence with epithalamion echoes;
And comes recurrent the undertone of the far surf,
Beating soft as the drowsed heart
Drifting to hollowed shores of sleep.

. . . In this fantastic universe of trees,
Earth, night, and the just-heard sea,
We ourselves are a singing world of joy, remote
From alien worlds of daylight, wheels turning, and mirrors,
Noise, and a hundred thousand hurrying faces,
Vexed minds scurrying in political, economic circles
Around ancient cages scrabbled, too, by Sumerians.
God-like, star-like, we gaze over empty conflicts,
Poised high over ruffled rights and wrongs
As a white gull above the waves' chopping.

Now does the moon, night's golden hind,
Wear on her bright, uplifted brow
Fresh antlers of the forked and spreading gum-twigs.
Moon-gold dissolves taut blackness of the trees,
Unfolding their clenched hands, as in your eyes
Fulfilment, soft-shining, dissolves all
Knotted reluctances into unbroken glowing
Of this, the second and last surrender,
Eros to hidden Psyche, spirit to serene oneness
As blood to fierce and prodigal union, appeasing
The druid circle with holy sacrifice
Out of the fire of the body's burning . . .

. . . At the cry of the cockerel dawn,
At the coming of the sun,
At the breaking of the bush-enchanted spell,
We shall touch long lips; loosen enfolding arms,
Let them fall again to widowed sides;
Look back, each to each, and the friendly gums.
We shall divide again into unflowering singleness,
Return to mad worlds of daylight, mirrors, wheels turning,
A hundred thousand horrible faces, jarred clangings,
Choppings of conscience, and scrabbled cages.

Yet no return can take enchantment of this hour
Twice-blest, eternal and memorial, since heart
Breeds wonders ungendered in mind's dry womb,
The dark blood remembers when the grey brain forgets.
Thoughts twinkle clear through centuried voids,
But love, not travelling, like these, unending rim
Of aeons revolving, pierces direct—a sun-flash—
To the moveless white eternity cored in encircling time.
Bleak winds of eroding ages bury our Babylons,
Yellowed waves of sand sweep over green gardens
Ambitiously hung on doloured slopes—no tragic
Avalanche, only the scorn of atomies silting;
And the forest is gone, and the unicorn loses
His spring horn, dies, leaves only bones in the desert.
Yet obelisk moments, carved by hammering passion,
Stand strongly, lifting their columned remembrance
Unchanged over debris of ruinous years.
Not only beauty, nor love alone, is born
This night—atonement for waste anarchies,
Balance for pains and dragging weight of nothingness—
But we, shepherds unknowing, under our bright stars
Have found fulfilling peace, birth of Immanuel faith;
And this, our joy, shall recur, star-shining, to light
The hid darkness of the deep self;
This spark, thrown from the infinite fire,
Shall burn, memorial, till death's last night
Bears us beyond the blood's wild singing,
Druidic gums and antlered moon.

THE MOONLIT DOORWAY

THE peacock-eye of the half-moon long since up;
the peacock-blue of the iridescent sky
moonlit to starless pallor; the scream of peacocks
across the bay from here mock night together
outside my windows—a wild, gritty scorn,
a jeer at memory, a blue-lit laughter
at man and me.
    Once, though, there was a doorway
set full of night and this same genial pallor
of moon-made sky-magic. Memory
does not give jeer for jeer. Memory's faithful
and so am I to memory—even tonight
when the imperial birds across the bay
scream out their scornful warning through the light
of blue darkness: 'She was white and golden
in that dark room the moonlight entered no more.
She was a pale woman lying there
whom you have never seen, whom you have known
well at night only—never well by day.'
And that mad scream through the doorway of my windows,
though less with distance, still cries out 'Beware.'
Beware of you, it says, your man's fallibility
in keeping faith. Beware of moons and midnights
lest the white body of the beloved suffer
a sad sky-change, and through that moonlit doorway
pass headlong into the hell of discontent,
the double hell of conscience and of scorn,
the final hell of hate. Beware, beware. . . .
    Of what I say. Of my heart? Of my mind?
Of the dark entry of this flood and flesh
into that younger and more innocent
flesh and blood, when the night was not far worn?
And I say, this was my fortune and delight,
and my long dreamed yet long withheld desire—
but more yet: my momentary destiny
that dream should harden into softest flesh
which, melting to the tongue, almost returns
to dream. This was my fortune, that her breasts
should stand upright and for an hour or more

tell me this body warmed and tensed and turned
with love to mine. This was my fine reward
for nothing more than kisses and caresses—
that in some hour or two there should have been
utter forgetfulness of me and life
in the profundity of face-to-face
against a doorway full of the moonlit sky,
silence, solitude, and she and I
alone and together.
　　　　Against the moonlit doorway is a tree,
flowered with a sparse but vigorous red by day
and black as a groping hand's lean skeleton
at night, when the moon's high. As I lay looking
I thought you had flown into it like a bird,
my child, my darling, silent and solitary
and watchful of the peacock treachery
of night, like a wary bird above the pool
of green lawn and new coming-together,
green knowledge and new understanding,
question, request, confession, answer, silence
as still as water. Then you were there again
with laughter in your mouth (I could not see
your clear eyes laughing in that silken darkness)
and in your hands a sudden secret cunning
as the desire and the will were mixed into
the slow and speechless deed itself. The tree
clawed kindly at the opal of the sky
with its red talons, and your own hands
are a mile away from you in space; and you
are a mile away from me, in space and time
and in intention. I, the servitor,
the bolder yet more humble of us two
who so astonishingly lie together,
am here no longer; I am in your body,
and, as the tree grown out of earth is earth,
so I am you, and you are my protection
against the tempests of the hated surface.
And into you I shall dissolve at last
with a great falling crash and sigh, contented.
　　　　With your cool graveness of a painted angel,
what do you think of, child, bedded in darkness

with your feet towards the peacock-coloured panel
of the open door? Just that the game is over?
Just that the night is cold and I am warm?
(This is what we were made for.) Just that the doorway
is beautiful in its silky moonlit splendour
slashed once with the dagger-sounds of a dog's barking
and once again with the unholy cry
of the royal birds impassioned by the night?
Tell me now—so long afterwards but so soon—
what you think lazily about, stretched here at ease
across my arm and shoulder and my heart.
Or yet—these are your own words—why should you speak?
I speak enough for both. My tongue's uncaged,
the padlock opened by a key of passion,
the door sprung wide, the wooing moon of love
luring it out and on, across the lawns,
down through the trees of your own silences
into the valley of your quiet body,
into the shadow of your lidded eyes,
between the moonlike mountains of your bosom,
through the whole world that's you, until it falls
silent, and with a sigh we almost sleep.

Through the tall moonlit doorway night looks in,
and once again the peacocks cry at us.

THE END OF DESIRE

A FLOODED fold of sarcenet
  Against her slender body sank,
Death-black, and beaded all with jet
  Across the pleasures of her flank.

The incense of a holy bowl
  Flowed round her knees till it did seem
That she was standing on the shoal
  Of some forbidden sunlit stream.

A little gong, far through the wall,
  Complained like one, deep sorrowing,
And, from the arras, I saw fall
  The woven swallow, fluttering;

While o'er the room there swam the breath
  Of roses on a trellised tree:
Loose ladies in pretended death
  Of sweet abandon to the bee.

Flames filled the hollows of my hands:
  Red blood rushed, hammering, round my heart,
Like mighty sleds when anvil bands
  Gape out, and from their holdings start.

No peace had I, and knew not where
  To find a solace that would kill
This pain of flesh so hard to bear,
  This sin of soul against the will.

But ever yet mine eyes would seek
  That golden woman built for love,
Whose either breast displayed the beak,
  Through pouted plumes, of Venus' dove:

Her heavy hair, as smoke blown down
  Athwart the fields of plenteousness;
Her folded lips, her placid frown,
  Her insolence of nakedness.

I took her closely, but while yet
  I trembled, vassal to my lust,
Lo!—Nothing but some sarcenet
  Deep-buried in a pile of dust.

THE DAMNATION OF BYRON

WHEN the great hero, adding to the charms
of genius and his scandals, left the light
stamped with the irresistible trade of arms,
the Hell of Women received him as their right.

Through the Infernal Fields he makes his way
playing again, but on a giant stage
his own Don Juan; pursuing day by day
Childe Harold's last astonishing pilgrimage.

It is the landscape of erotic dreams:
the dim, brown plains, the country without air
or tenderness of trees by hidden streams,
but cactus or euphorbia here and there

thrusts up its monstrous phallus at the sky.
And moving against this silvered, lustrous green
like a pink larva over the whole dry
savannah of hell, the bodies of women are seen.

And at his coming all their beauties stir
mysterious like the freshening of a rose;
as, the incomparable connoisseur,
pale and serene across their world he goes

always there rises glowing in his path
superb and sensual, in the light that pours
a tarnished glory on the soil of death,
this leafless nakedness of tropic flowers;

the female body's impersonal charm, the curves
of a young head poised on its gracious stalk.
The idiom of her gesture he observes,
that tender dislocation of her walk.

Held in his brain's deep lupanar they float,
the tapering trunk, the pure vase of the hips,
the breasts, the breasts to which the hands go out
instinctive, the adoring finger tips,

148

the thighs incurved, the skin misted with light,
the mouth repeating its own rich circumflex . . .
At first he moves and breathes in his delight
drowned in the brute somnambulism of sex.

He is a kind of symbol of the male:
as a great bull, stiffly, deliberately
crosses his paddock, lashing his brutal tail,
the sullen engine of fecundity,

so, in his first youth and his first desire,
his air of pride and the immortal bloom,
once more he sets the feminine world on fire,
passing in his romantic blaze of gloom.

Prodigious vigour flowers new in him:
each morning nerves him with heroic lust.
His thoughts are women, he breathes, is clothed
        with them,
he sinks on something female in the dust.

He has them all, all the menagerie
of race, the subtle stimulus of shapes:
Negresses in their first nubility
with the sad eyes and muzzles of young apes,

vast Scandinavian divinities
superbly modelled, for all their cowlike air,
the pale bread of their bellies magnificent rise
from the blond triangle of pubic hair,

and slender girls with delicate golden shanks
and elongated skulls from lost Peru . . .
and sensual emphasis of the Spaniard's flanks,
and the callipygous haunches of the Jew . . .

Dancers and whores, bluestockings, countesses,
types of La Fornarina and Caroline Lamb,
all the seductions of all mistresses,
the savage, the sentimental and the sham . . .

L

And yet he is alone. At first he feels
nothing above the tumult of his blood,
while through his veins like the slow pox there steals
the deep significance of his solitude.

And from this feeling without haste or pause
vengeance predestined sharpens, bit by bit;
as lust its anaesthesia withdraws
the force of his damnation grows from it.

Grows as the mind wakes, inexorably
the critic, the thinker, the invincible
intelligence at last detached and free
wakes, and he knows . . . He knows he is in hell.

And there begins in him that horrible thing
clairvoyance, the cruel nightmare of escape:
He seeks companions: but they only bring
wet kisses and voluptuous legs agape.

He longs for the companionship of men,
their sexless friendliness. He cannot live
'like the gods in Lucretius once again'
nor ever in woman's wit and charm forgive

the taint of the pervading feminine.
Yet always to this nausea he returns
from his own mind—the emptiness within
of the professional lover—As he learns

how even his own society has become
a horror, a loneliness he cannot bear,
the last stage of Don Juan's martyrdom,
the last supreme resources of despair

appear, and brutally lucid he descends
simply to treat them as The Enemy.
His lust becomes revenge, his ardour lends
insatiable pleasure to his insanity.

As he exhausts himself in the delights
of torture, gormandising in their pain,
hate eats his features out: it seethes and bites
like a slow acid. It destroys his brain.

Yet this resource betrays him, even this,
for like tormented demons, they adore
their torment. They revere like savages
the god's ferocity with lascivious awe.

Until, neurotic, hounded by strange fears,
at last his journey changes to a flight.
Delirious, broken, fugitive, he hears
marching and countermarching in the night,

the panic of vague terrors closing in:
whichever way he turns he hears them come.
Far off immeasurable steps begin,
far off the ominous mumble of a drum,

and from the bounds of that dim listening land
approaches with her grave incessant tread
the Eternal Goddess in whose placid hand
are all the happy and all the rebellious dead.

Before her now he stands and makes his prayer
for that oblivion of the Second Death . . .
when suddenly those majestic breasts all bare
riding the tranquil motion of her breath

reveal the body of her divinity:
the torso spread marmoreal, his eyes
downwards uncover its mighty line and see
darkness dividing those prodigious thighs.

There as he stares, slowly she smiles at him . . .
And the great hero, mad with the terrible
madness of souls turns fleeing, while the dim
plains heave with the immense derision of Hell.

O WHITE WIND

O WHITE wind, numbing the world
to a mask of suffering hate!
and thy goblin pipes have skirl'd
all night, at my broken gate.

O heart, be hidden and kept
in a half-light colour'd and warm,
and call on thy dreams that have slept
to charm thee from hate and harm.

They are gone, for I might not keep;
my sense is beaten and dinn'd:
there is no peace but a gray sleep
in the pause of the wind.

THE DICE WERE LOADED

THE dice were loaded full and well
The dreadful night that I was born,
The devils danced a tarantelle,
The whimpering plovers fled the corn.

A fox that hunted hungry food
Lifted his head in ravaged cry;
A shadow ran from out the wood,
In after years that shade was I.

I trod the dark mile all alone,
I trod it lone through all the years;
And but the midnight heard my moan,
And but the bitter earth my tears.

I make no plaint, I make no cry,
No back look give to yesterday;
For, where I saw the hazard lie,
I played the game they bid me play.

And now I hang upon a tree,
My lovely body all forlorn;
The loaded dice were thrown for me,
Upon the night that I was born.

AT MANLY

Down below the combers drape
Rocks with bridal finery,
To the northward cape on cape
Thrusts a slavered snout to sea.

Peace, is there no peace?
On the beach
The waves are breaking
Without cease,
In the glare
The roofs are shaking.

Peace, is there no peace?
On the rocks
The sea is wearing
Without cease,
At the pines
The wind is tearing.

Peace, is there no peace?
In the life
The sense is shaking
Without cease,
On the flesh
The soul is breaking.

Peace, is there no peace?
At the nerves
The mind is tearing
Without cease,
On the man
The world is wearing.

Peace?
Who will to live
They wish no peace
That death can give.

RES PUBLICA

THEY bled a bullock, and stripped the hide,
Cast to the dogs what they could not use;
Tanned the skin that the sun had dried,
And made the leather for Caesar's shoes.

A shivering lamb was shorn in Spain;
The wool was teased and combed and dressed.
They washed it clean of the pasture stain,
And wove the toga for Caesar's breast.

A pig that rooted acorns saw
The shrub resent as they plucked the bough,
And watched the shadows of men withdraw
Bearing the laurel for Caesar's brow.

They dug the metal to fill the mould,
And fed the flame in a place apart,
Ground the edge when the steel was cold,
And made the dagger for Caesar's heart.

MONTORO'S SONG AGAINST COUNT ALVARO
DE LUNA, HIGH CONSTABLE OF CASTILE

(From the Spanish of E. Marquina)

'KING, a flock is feeding
down the cliff unheeding
   and upon the hill,
with your crook to shepherd it. . . .'
—It is yours, O Favourite.
   Ask for what you will.

'In your crown a jewel
blazes fierce and cruel—
   kingship to fulfil.
Such a royal stone is it. . . .'
—It is yours, O Favourite.
   Ask for what you will.

'King, see, your rejected
sceptre lies neglected
   on the throne-steps still.
Long you have forgotten it. . . .'
—It is yours, O Favourite.
   Ask for what you will.

'King, in kingly measure
I have spent my treasure,
   haste my stores to fill!
Be my Envoy leal and fit—'
—I shall do so, Favourite.
   Ask for what you will.

'King, tell me I am dreaming;
I see the tapers gleaming;
   a scaffold boding ill
with the headsman swart by it—'
—It is yours, O Favourite,
   ask for what you will.

FEATHERS

LET us put feathers
in our hair and dance
and touch the moon with a feather.
Let us throw back our heads and chant
insolent phrasing
for a stately measure.
Let us pretend the moon is silver
not a grey pocked cast,
that we are white with pleasure.
Let us forget that fatigue
has stolen our days,
oblique, capricious,
with a monkey's claws.
Let us forget that terror creaks
above and below
on empty stairs:
that blood is old on the streets
and the white clock's fears
are counted and thrown away
until the house is grey
with wild geese feathers.

Let us put feathers in our hair
and dance
and touch the lips
with a feather:
let us rehearse our conversations
approaching briefly
with the fingertips:

You see the moon's new silver
on the rain-washed dusk,
a wind that is bent across
a pigeon's wings.
With rapt ineptitude
the night bird sings
while we who are tiger-striped
for night and day
do not care to sing,
we prey . . .

Let us with all the rare
artifices of dim ceremony
embrace and descend with care
the murmurous stairs
declining into night.
Let us descend to hide
in the long wave's shadow
and bow three times
to touch the earth
with fingers of willow.

From THE VICTORIA MARKETS RECOLLECTED IN TRANQUILLITY

I

Winds are bleak, stars are bright,
Loads lumber along the night:
Looming, ghastly white,
A towering truck of cauliflowers sways
Out of the dark, roped over and packed tight
Like faces of a crowd of football jays.

The roads come in, roads dark and long,
To the knock of hubs and a sleepy song.
Heidelberg, Point Nepean, White Horse,
Flemington, Keilor, Dandenong,
Into the centre from the source.

Rocking in their seats
The worn-out drivers droop
When dawn stirs in the streets
And the moon's a silver hoop;
Come rumbling into the silent mart,
To put their treasure at its heart,
Waggons, lorries, a lame Ford bus,
Like ants along the arms of an octopus
Whose body is all one mouth; that pays them hard
And drives them back with less than a slave's reward.

When Batman first at Heaven's command
Said, 'This is the place for a peanut-stand.'
It must have been grand!

II

'Cheap to-day, lady; cheap to-day!'
Jostling water-melons roll
From fountains of Earth's mothering soul.
Tumbling from box and tray
Rosy, cascading apples play
Each with a glowing aureole
Caught from a split sun-ray.

'Cheap to-day, lady, cheap to-day.'
Hook the carcases from the dray!
(Where the dun bees hunt in droves
Apples ripen in the groves.)

An old horse broods in a Chinaman's cart
While from the throbbing mart
Go cheese and celery, pears and jam
In barrow, basket, bag or pram
To the last dram the purse affords—
Food, food for the hordes.

Shuffling in the driven crush
The souls and the bodies cry,
Rich and poor, skimped and flush,
'Spend or perish. Buy or die!'

Food, food for the hordes!
Turksheads tumble on the boards.

.   .   .   .   .

Along the shadows furtive, lone,
The unwashed terrier carries his week-end bone.
An old horse with a pointed hip
And dangling disillusioned under-lip
Stands in a harvest-home of cabbage leaves
And grieves.
A lady by a petrol case,
With a far-off wounded look in her face
Says, in a voice of uncertain pitch,
'Muffins' or 'crumpets', I'm not sure which.
A pavement battler whines with half a sob,
'Ain't anybody got a bloody bob?'
Haunted by mortgages and overdrafts
The old horse droops between the shafts.
A smiling Chinaman upends a bag
And spills upon the bench with thunder-thud
(A nearby urchin trilling the newest rag)
Potatoes caked with loamy native mud.

160

Andean pinnacles of labelled jam.
The melting succulence of two-toothed lamb.
The little bands of hemp that truss
The succulent asparagus
That stands like tiny sheaves of purple wheat
Ready to eat!
Huge and alluring hams and rashered swine
In circular repetitive design.
Gobbling turkeys and ducks in crates,
Pups in baskets and trays of eggs;
A birdman turns and gloomily relates
His woes to a girl with impossible legs.

When Batman first at Heaven's command
Stuck flag-staffs in this sacred strand . . .
We'll leave all that to the local band.

. . . . . .

THE RETURN FROM THE FREUDIAN ISLANDS

WHEN they heard Sigmund the Saviour in these coasts
the islanders were very much impressed;
abandoned the worship of their fathers' ghosts
and dedicated temples to their guest,

shocked and delighted as the saint revealed
the unacknowledged body and made them see
suppressed by corsets, morbidly concealed,
in cotton combinations, neck to knee,

how it bred night-sweats, the disease of shame,
corns, fluxions, baldness and the sense of sin,
how clothes to the Analytic Eye became
fantasies, furtive symbols of the skin.

At first the doctrine took them all by storm;
urged to be stark, they peeled as they were told;
forgetting their rags had also kept them warm
for the island climate is often extremely cold.

And if the old, the wry, the ugly shared
some natural reluctance to begin it,
enthusiasts all, the young at once declared
their Brave Nude world, that had such people in it.

Till some discovered that stripping to the buff
only exposed the symbol of The Hide:
its sinister pun unmasked, it must come off,
the saint must preach The Visible Inside!

The saint, though somewhat startled at this view,
trapped by the logic of his gospel, spent
some time in prayer, and in a week or two,
to demonstrate the new experiment,

breastless and bald, with ribbed arms, lashless eyes,
in intricate bandages of human meat,
with delicate ripple and bulge of muscled thighs,
the first skinned girl walked primly down the street.

Though there were many to admire her charms:
the strappings and flexures of twig-like toes, the skeins
and twisted sensitive cables of her arms,
the pectoral fans, the netting of nerves and veins:

yet those who followed her example found
one lack—till Sigmund undertook to prove
how much their late behaviour centred round
a common skin disease they had called love.

And for a time they thoroughly enjoyed
the brisk intolerance of the purified
in sects and schisms before The Holy Freud
self-torn—while lesser saints were deified.

Till Faith, which never can let well alone,
from heresy and counter-heresy
prompted the saint to bare beneath the bone
The Ultimate Visceral Reality.

Long time he mused before The Sacred Id,
long prayed, before he finally began,
and purged, impersonal, uninhibited,
produced at last The Basic Freudian Man.

At the Fertility Festival that year
the skinned men blushed to see the skeleton,
a bone-cage filled with female guts appear
tottering before them in the midday sun.

Its slats and levering rods they saw, the full
cogged horseshoe grin of two and thirty teeth,
the frantic eyeballs swivelling in the skull,
the swagging human umbles underneath,

the soft wet mottled granite of the lung
bulge and collapse, the liver worn askew
jauntily quiver, the plump intestines hung
in glistening loops and bolsters in their view,

and clear through gut and bowel the mashy chyme
churn downward; jelled in its transparent sheath
the scowling fœtus tethered, and the time
bomb tumour set unguessed its budded death.

And while for them with mannequin grace she swayed
her pelvis, Sigmund, so that none should miss
the beauty of the new world he had made
explained The Triumph of Analysis:

Pimples and cramps now shed with pelt and thews,
no dreams to fright, no visions to trouble them,
for, where the death-wish and self-knowledge fuse,
they had at last The Human L.C.M. . . .

Here the saint paused, looked modestly at the ground
and waited for their plaudits to begin.
And waited . . . There was nothing! A faint, dry
    sound
as first a poet buttoned on his skin.

THE BAYONET

THAT's not a broom you're using, soldier.

Handle your rifle as though it were such—
Left breast! Right breast! Navel! Groin!
Butt of the rifle into the crutch!
Now—where the throat and thorax join!

The captain says you'll make a soldier.

(Once I bayoneted a Senegalese
In Syrian moonlight . . .
He didn't scream much after the first thrust,
Only moaned;
And his limbs jerked in the dust
For all the world like a black spider
Impaled on a blued-steel pin.

It isn't pleasant to see men
Scribbling their agony in dirt.

I thrust again, teeth bared,
A long-point to the throat
It was this time:
And his knees shot to his chin,
Relaxed . . .
And the limbs were still.)

Point and parry, port and thrust!
Make your opponent feel your might!
Yell, man! Scream, man! Wake your lust!
On guard! Withdraw! My God, man . . .
        fight!

The captain says I'll make a soldier.

M

THE TREE AT POST 4

I AM the first, of all the rancorous men
hating this blazing desert of a post,
to find you here, my darling, changed like Daphne
into a tree, and then transformed again
to your own distant self.
         The white trunk
that soars so smoothly upward and is lost
in frozen clouds of leaves against the moon
is yours, as once I saw you stilled by a thought
above the golden candle flame that bathed you
from throat to knees in friendly, stirring light
against the warm room's velvet depth of night.
And these immaculate limbs—they too are yours,
enfolding and compassioning my heart
within their rounded immobility,
lit from below, carved with a lover's art
to shadowless grace. I recognize them well,
salute them with a sigh, and dare not look
too long, lest in the magic of the hour
time be turned backward, and the shining tree
become yourself, stripped bare and pale, and still
caught in a thought, arrested in this pose
above a candle long since burnt away
and drowned in shadows in a room now empty.
Imagination, like an untimely rose,
blows out and withers in this garish light
about Post 4. Only the tree will stay
steady and haunting me till dawn puts out
the icy globes, and warms its limbs with day.

THESE MEN

MEN moving in a trench, in the clear noon,
  Whetting their steel within the crumbling earth;
Men, moving in a trench 'neath a new moon
  That smiles with a slit mouth and has no mirth;
Men moving in a trench in the grey morn,
  Lifting bodies on their clotted frames;
Men with narrow mouths thin-carved in scorn
  That twist and fumble strangely at dead names.

· · · · · ·

These men know life—know death a little more.
  These men see paths and ends, and see
Beyond some swinging open door
  Into eternity.

IN THE TRENCH

EVERY night I sleep,
   And every night I dream
That I'm strolling with my sheep
   By the old stream.

Every morn I wake,
   And every morn I stand
And watch the shrapnel break
   On the smashed land.

Some night I'll fall asleep,
   And will not wake at dawn.
I'll lie and feed my sheep
   On a green Lawn.

MEN IN GREEN

Oh, there were fifteen men in green,
Each with a tommy-gun,
Who leapt into my plane at dawn;
We rose to meet the sun.

We set our course towards the east
And climbed into the day
Till the ribbed jungle underneath
Like a giant fossil lay.

We climbed towards the distant range
Where two white paws of cloud
Clutched at the shoulders of the pass;
The green men laughed aloud.

They did not fear the ape-like cloud
That climbed the mountain crest
And hung from twisted ropes of air
With thunder in their breast.

They did not fear the summer's sun
In whose hot centre lie
A hundred hissing cannon shells
For the unwatchful eye.

And when on Dobadura's field
We landed, each man raised
His thumb towards the open sky;
But to their right I gazed.

For fifteen men in jungle green
Rose from the kunai grass
And came towards the plane. My men
In silence watched them pass;
It seemed they looked upon themselves
In Time's prophetic glass.

Oh, there were some leaned on a stick
And some on stretchers lay,
But few walked on their own two feet
In the early green of day.

They had not feared the ape-like cloud
That climbed the mountain crest;
They had not feared the summer's sun
With bullets for their breast.

Their eyes were bright, their looks were dull,
Their skin had turned to clay.
Nature had met them in the night
And stalked them in the day.

And I think still of men in green
On the Soputa track
With fifteen spitting tommy-guns
To keep a jungle back.

THE MOUNTAIN

THE mountain he flew over did not want him,
Loose with age, the shaggy cliffs looked down
While webbed in fire the angels' right was lent him
To pass the mighty without fear and frown.

Wanting no lover, being alive sufficed
To see death powerless in the waste of snow.
The helmeted brain knew mastery and faced
All hate quiescent in the earth below.

Time rested on his wrist, while he ignored
Designs created in a loveless room,
That waiting round the aerodrome he neared
Could rescue no one lonely with his doom.

His walking sprung with moss, he stands
Minute beside the hard and polished trees,
Hearing how a bird-call whips the cliffs and winds
The rocks to clasp no mercy at their knees.

BEACH BURIAL

Softly and humbly to the Gulf of Arabs
The convoys of dead sailors come;
At night they sway and wander in the waters far under,
But morning rolls them in the foam.

Between the sob and clubbing of the gunfire
Someone, it seems, has time for this,
To pluck them from the shallows and bury them in burrows
And tread the sand upon their nakedness;

And each cross, the driven stake of tidewood,
Bears the last signature of men,
Written with such perplexity, with such bewildered pity,
The words choke as they begin—

'*Unknown seaman*'—the ghostly pencil
Wavers and fades, the purple drips,
The breath of the wet season has washed their inscriptions
As blue as drowned men's lips,

Dead seamen, gone in search of the same landfall,
Whether as enemies they fought,
Or fought with us, or neither; the sand joins them together,
Enlisted on the other front.

1914

THE sparrow has gone home into the tree;
And the belled cattle, vague and pensive-eyed,
Drowse in the twilight, to the red cliffside
Comes but a faded murmur of the sea.
Comes down the night; comes down reluctantly
The mist upon the hill whence soon shall glide
A pale and bashful moon; with arms spread wide
Affrighted pixies seek the dark from me.

These shall return: the mountains and the haze,
The blue lobelias ledging all the lawns,
The pixies, the lost roads and the sun-blaze,
These waters surge to-morrow to this shore—
All these things shall return with other dawns
But pity to the hearts of men no more.

THE CHILDREN MARCH

THE children of the world are on the march
From the dangerous cots, the nurseries ringed with fire,
The poisoned toys, the playgrounds pitted
With bomb craters and shrapnel strewn about;
From the whips, the iron bars, the guns' great shout,
The malevolent teachers and the lethal sports
Played on the ruined fields fenced by red wires.

The children of the world are on the march
With the doll and the school-bag to safe quarters,
The temporary haven, the impermanent home;
Nightly turning their thoughts to the forsaken hearth,
The wandering, wondering children of the world
March on the sea and land and crowded air—
The unsmiling sons, the sad bewildered daughters.

LAMENT

SIGH, wind in the pine;
River, weep as you flow;
Terrible things were done
Long, long ago.

In daylight golden and mild
After the night of Glencoe
They found the hand of a child
Lying upon the snow.

Lopped by the sword to the ground
Or torn by wolf or fox,
That was the snowdrop they found
Among the granite rocks.

Oh, life is fierce and wild
And the heart of the earth is stone,
And the hand of a murdered child
Will not bear thinking on.

Sigh, wind in the pine,
Cover it over with snow;
But terrible things were done
Long, long ago.

RETURNED SOLDIER

I PUT him on the train in Albury
The night he went to take his boat, and he,
Swinging aboard, called gaily, 'Don't forget,
I'll dodge them all and be a farmer yet,
And raise, for every bullet that goes by,
A stalk of wheat, red-gold and shoulder high,
Three hundred acres, lad!' And then the train
Was gone. The night was loud with frogs again.

And five years later, one November day,
I walked with Barry down the stooks of hay
Light yellow in the sun, and on them fluttered
Rosellas red as apples. Barry muttered
Half shyly as we faced the level wheat:
'One good foot left of what was once two feet,
One lung just fair, and one unclouded eye;
But all those years I heard them whining by
And in the mud I chuckled to remember
How wheat turns copper and gold in late November.'
He smiled, and then I knew what charm had brought
Him safely past the 'world's great snare,' uncaught.

THE FARMER REMEMBERS THE SOMME

WILL they never fade or pass!
The mud, and the misty figures endlessly coming
In file through the foul morass,
And the grey flood-water lipping the reeds and grass,
And the steel wings drumming.

The hills are bright in the sun:
There's nothing changed or marred in the well-known
    places;
When work for the day is done
There's talk, and quiet laughter, and gleams of fun
On the old folks' faces.

I have returned to these:
The farm, and the kindly Bush, and the young calves
    lowing;
But all that my mind sees
Is a quaking bog in a mist—stark, snapped trees,
And the dark Somme flowing.

CENOTAPH

WHEN it was dark in Martin Place,
  And when all sound was still,
I thought I saw a ravaged face
  Stare blindly up the hill.

I thought I heard a ringing sound
  Of hoofbeats in the street,
And from the pavement all around
  The stamp of horses' feet.

And, as I stood in reverie,
  Surely I heard a cry;
'The Legions of Eternity,
  Lord God, are riding by!

'The Legions of Eternity
  Are riding down the years
To trumpet to posterity
  A tale to tell in tears,

'To tell in unashamed tears
  Of triumph over pain,
How young men doffed their cloak of fears
  That Man might rise again.

'Lord, some rode in from Mittagong,
  Some from the Golden Mile,
And some lived hard, but few lived long
  Who joined the Desert File.

'The gates of Jericho were wide
  To greet us—years ago;
But now forlorn, as ghosts we ride
  Who rode to Jericho.

'Lord, now the ranks are mostly gaps,
  The squadron mostly holes,
For Gabriel long since blew *Taps*
  And gathered up our souls.

'In gallant company we rode,
　Nor knew the cause we made,
And seed to spring eternal sowed,
　Nor was its measure weighed.

'The enemy we knew was man,
　Yet Man we sought to free;
Lord, now we know our heart's blood ran
　For ends we could not see—

'That futile strife to futile gain
　Might share with us a grave,
And those who follow not disdain
　That which we strove to save.

'Now for our souls let all men pray,
　Hearing our tale again,
That the red dead who pass this way
　May not have died in vain.

'*Ora pro nobis!*—hear our cry
　Who died a world away,
The Shining Legion riding by,
　Non nobis solum, say.'

Lord, it was dark in Martin Place,
　And silence seemed more still.
Surely I saw a ravaged face
　Stare blindly up the hill.

TITLES AND AUTHORS
AUTHORS AND TITLES
BIOGRAPHIES

N

TITLES AND AUTHORS

TITLES AND AUTHORS

TITLES AND AUTHORS

AUTHORS AND TITLES

AUTHORS AND TITLES

Page

BIOGRAPHIES

ALLEN, LESLIE HOLDSWORTH, M.A. (Syd.), Ph.D. (Leipzig), 1879. Born at Maryborough, Vic. Educated at Newington College and the Universities of Sydney and Leipzig, to the latter of which he won a travelling scholarship. Lecturer Emeritus in English and Classics at Canberra University College and chairman of the Commonwealth Book Censorship Committee. Widower. Publications include *Billy Bubbles, Child Songs*, 1920; *Phaedra and Other Poems*, 1921; *Araby and Other Poems*, 1924; *Patria*, 1941; and two of the plays contained in *Three Plays by Frederic Hebbel* (trans.), 1914.

ANDERSON, ETHEL LOUISE, *née* Mason.
Born in England of Australian parents and educated at the Church of England Girls' Grammar School, Sydney. Has contributed to various British and American as well as Australian periodicals. Publications: *Squatter's Luck*, 1942; *Sunday at Yarralumla*, 1946; also collections of sketches and short stories, and a novel.

BRENNAN, CHRISTOPHER JOHN, M.A. (Syd.), 1870-1932.
Born in Sydney. Educated at Riverview and the University of Sydney, where he won a travelling scholarship to the University of Berlin. In Germany he studied German romanticism and French symbolism but did not sit for a doctorate. On return to Sydney he became cataloguer at the Public Library of N.S.W. He married, and later lectured in various subjects at the University and in 1920 became Professor of Comparative Literature. In 1925 he was asked to resign, and during the remainder of his life coached at intervals and was awarded a small Commonwealth pension. Publications: *XVIII Poems*, 1897; *XXI Poems*, 1897; *Poems*, 1914; *A Chant of Doom*, 1918; and (with J. Le G. Brereton) *A Mask*, 1913. In 1938 *Twenty-Three Poems*, a selection, partly from manuscript, was published by the Australian Limited Editions Society, Sydney.

CAMPBELL, DAVID, 1915.
Born at Ellerslie station, near Adelong, N.S.W. Educated at The King's School, Sydney, where he was captain of the school and prominent in athletics, and at Cambridge, from which he represented England against Ireland and Wales in football. In 1938 he returned to Australia. At the outbreak of war he joined

the R.A.A.F., became a wing commander and won a D.F.C. and Bar. He is now a farmer. Married. Publication: *Speak With the Sun*, 1949.

CHEYNE, IRENE, 1885.

Born at Wangaratta, Vic., of parents who were also Australian-born and had a number of literary connections in England. Educated at the Brigidine Convent, Echuca, Vic. Publications: Several novels, but no book of verse so far.

CHRISTESEN, CLEMENT (BYRNE), 1912.

Born at Townsville, Q., and educated at state schools and the University of Queensland. Athletics 'Blue'. Has been a publicist for the Queensland government, a University Extension lecturer, a lecturer for the Commonwealth Literary Fund, a member of the sub-editorial staffs of Australian and London newspapers and a radio feature writer, and is now manager and editor in Australia for William Heinemann Ltd. Founder and editor of *Meanjin*. Married. Publications include *North Coast*, 1943; *South Coast*, 1944; *Dirge and Lyrics*, 1945; and several travel books. Also edited a prose anthology, *Australian Heritage*, 1949.

DEVANEY, JAMES (MARTIN), 1890.

Born at Bendigo, Vic., and educated at St. Joseph's College, Sydney. Literary critic, freelance journalist, teacher; has lectured at several universities for the Commonwealth Literary Fund. Married. Publications: *Poems*, 1950, which collected poems from several former books; *Shaw Neilson*, a biography, 1944; *Unpublished Poems of Shaw Neilson* (ed.), 1947; and several novels.

DOBSON, ROSEMARY (DE BRISSAC, Mrs A. T. Bolton), 1920.

Born in Sydney. Educated at Frensham, Mittagong, N.S.W., and also studied art in Sydney. Taught art and art appreciation at Frensham, and is now on the editorial staff of Angus and Robertson Ltd., Sydney. Publications: *In a Convex Mirror*, 1944; and *The Ship of Ice*, 1948, whose title-poem won first prize in the *Sydney Morning Herald's* verse competition for 1947. Edited *Australian Poetry, 1949-50*.

DUTTON, GEOFFREY (PIERS HENRY), 1922.

Born at Kapunda, S.A., and educated at Geelong Grammar School, Vic., and the University of Oxford. During the second World War was a flight lieutenant in the R.A.A.F. Now lives in England, but gives his 'permanent address' as Kapunda, S.A. Publications: *Night Flight and Sunrise*, 1944; and a novel, *The Mortal and the Marble*, 1950.

DYSON, WILL (WILLIAM HENRY), 1880-1938.
Born near Ballarat, Vic. Began drawing for the *Bulletin* at nineteen, and in 1910 went to London and became one of the most famous cartoonists of the day; was among the principal artists with the A.I.F. in the first World War. Married in 1910 Ruby Lindsay (sister of Norman Lindsay), who died in 1919. Publications include *Poems in Memory of a Wife*, 1919; and *Kultur Cartoons*, 1915; *Australia at War*, 1918; *An Artist Among the Bankers*, 1933.

'E', *see* FULLERTON, MARY.

FILSON, MRS A. J., *see* 'RICKETTY KATE'.

FITZGERALD, ROBERT DAVID, O.B.E., 1902.
Born at Hunter's Hill, N.S.W. Educated at Sydney Grammar School and the University of Sydney (Faculty of Science), but left without taking a degree. Qualified as a land surveyor in 1925, and has practised his profession in Fiji and various parts of N.S.W.; at present a senior surveyor in the Department of the Interior, Sydney. Married. Publications: *To Meet the Sun*, 1929 (this included the contents of a previous booklet, *The Greater Apollo*), and *Moonlight Acre*, 1938. This was awarded the gold medal of the Australian Literature Society for the best book of verse of the year; it contained 'Essay on Memory', which won the sesquicentenary prize poem competition. Two more books of verse, *This Night's Orbit* and *Between Two Tides*, are in preparation. Edited *Australian Poetry, 1942*.

FITZPATRICK, BRIAN (CHARLES), M.A., 1905.
Born at Warrnambool, Vic., and educated at Essendon High School and the University of Melbourne. Scholar, publisher, journalist; editor of *The Australian News-Review*; Research Fellow and, later, Research Officer in the School of History, University of Melbourne. Publications include *Songs and Poems*, 1931; and *British Imperialism and Australia 1783-1833*, 1939; and *The British Empire in Australia 1834-1939*, 1941.

FULLERTON, MARY (ELIZABETH), 'E', 1868-1946.
Born in Gippsland, Vic., but lived in London after 1921. Publications include *Moods and Melodies*, 1908; *The Breaking Furrow*, 1921; *Bark House Days* (essays and sketches), 1921;

and several novels, besides two books of verse signed 'E', which were written and published after she had taken up her permanent residence in England.

GELLERT, LEON, 1892.
Born at Walkerville, S.A., and educated at Adelaide High School and the University of Adelaide. Served in the A.I.F. in the first World War from the Gallipoli landing onward. Was director and co-editor of *Art in Australia* and editor of *The Home*, and is now on the literary staff of the *Sydney Morning Herald*. Married. Publications include *Songs of a Campaign*, 1917; *The Isle of San*, 1919; and *Desperate Measures*, 1929.

GILMORE, DAME MARY (JEAN), *née* Cameron, D.B.E., 1865.
Born near Goulburn, N.S.W.; father Highland, mother Australian. Taught in N.S.W. country schools and afterwards became one of the leaders of the New Australia colony in Paraguay, where she married. In 1908 founded and for many years edited the Woman's Page in the Sydney *Worker*. Publications: *Selected Verse*, 1948, which collected poems from several former books; *Hound of the Road* (reminiscent essays), and several books of reminiscence.

GRANO, PAUL LANGTON, LL.B. (Melb.), 1894.
Born at Ararat, Vic. Educated at St. Patrick's College, Ballarat, and the University of Melbourne. After a few years' legal practice he followed various occupations, and is now on the staff of the Queensland Main Roads Commission. Publications: *Poems New and Old*, 1945, which collected poems from several earlier books; also edited a Catholic verse anthology, *Witness to the Stars*, 1946.

HARFORD, LESBIA (VENNER), *née* Keogh, B.A., LL.B. (Melb.), 1891-1927. Born in Melbourne and educated at the Sacred Heart Convent, Melbourne, and the University of Melbourne. She taught, studied law and worked in a lawyer's office in Sydney and Melbourne, joined the I.W.W., and became a factory hand in order to investigate the lives of the poor. Publication: *Poems*, 1941.

HARRIS, MAX (MAXWELL HENRY), 1921.
Born in Adelaide and educated at St. Peter's College and the University of Adelaide. Has been an Economics Research Officer, publisher and bookseller. While an undergraduate, founded and edited *Angry Penguins*, a vigorous magazine which

had many of the merits and defects of adolescence. Married. Publications: *The Gift of Blood*, 1940; *Dramas from the Sky*, 1942; and a novel.

HART-SMITH, WILLIAM, 1911.
Born in England, and educated in England, Scotland and New Zealand. Served in the A.I.F. in the second World War, and has since followed various occupations, including those of radio mechanic, radio copywriter and freelance journalist. Is now Tutor-Organizer for Adult Education in Canterbury, N.Z. Married. Publications include *Columbus Goes West*, 1943, and *Christopher Columbus*, 1948.

HASLUCK, PAUL (MEERNAA CAEDWALLA), M.A. (W.A.), 1905. Born in Fremantle, W.A., and educated at W.A. state schools and the University of Western Australia. Has been a journalist, honorary secretary of the Western Australian Historical Society, Reader in History at the University of Western Australia, and for several years engaged on the political volume of the history of Australia in the second World War. Has always been particularly interested in the Australian aborigine and his problems. Was a member of the Department of External Affairs and of a number of important international commissions and committees, and is now Minister for Territories in the Commonwealth government. Married. Publications include *Into the Desert*, 1939 and *Our Southern Half-Castes*, 1938; *Black Australians*, 1942, and *Workshop of Security*, 1948.

HOPE, ALEC (DERWENT), B.A. (Syd. and Oxon), 1907.
Born at Cooma, N.S.W. Educated at Bathurst and Fort Street High Schools and at the Universities of Sydney and Oxford, to the latter of which he won a travelling scholarship. Was a teacher and vocational psychologist, and a lecturer in English at the Sydney Teachers' College and the University of Melbourne, and is now Professor of English at the Canberra University College. Married. He has published one or two booklets and a number of critical articles in Australian periodicals, but so far no book of verse.

HOPEGOOD, OLIVE, *née* Clucas (Mrs G. J. H. Ebbinge Wubben). Born in W.A., of Manx parentage on one side and Irish on the other. Educated in Perth, W.A. Has been librarian and journalist.

HOPEGOOD, PETER, 1891.
Born in England, and educated at Dover College, Aspatria Agricultural College and Brighton Art School. Spent five years

O

in the Canadian backblocks and served with a British regiment in the first World War. Became a freelance journalist and illustrator. Came out to Australia for health reasons in 1924, spent several years in the Western Australian bush and tried pearling, but now lives in Sydney. Publications include *Circus at World's End*, 1947, which collected poems from previous books; and the autobiographical *Peter Lecky, By Himself*, 1935.

HOWARTH, ROBERT GUY, B.A. (Syd.), B.Litt. (Oxon), 1906. Born at Tenterfield, N.S.W. Educated at Fort Street High School and the Universities of Sydney and Oxford, to the latter of which he won a travelling scholarship. Reader in English at the University of Sydney, member of the Advisory Board of the Commonwealth Literary Fund, President of the Sydney Branch of the English Association, and founder and editor of *Southerly*. Married. Publications: *Spright and Geist*, 1944, and *Involuntaries*, 1948. He also edited *Australian Poetry, 1944*, and is the author of a book of essays, *Literary Particles*, 1946; editor of a number of works of scholarship in English literature, and of several collections by Australian poets and prose writers.

INGAMELLS, REX (REGINALD CHARLES), 1913. Born at Orroroo, S.A., and educated at S.A. state schools and the University of Adelaide. Has hiked from Adelaide to Melbourne, spent four seasons fruit-picking along the Murray and travelled in a schooner trading along the South Australian coast. Has been a schoolteacher and is now a publisher's traveller. Founded the Jindyworobak Club and is general editor of its publications. Publications include *Selected Poems*, 1944, which collected poems from a number of previous books; *Yera*, 1945; *Come Walkabout*, 1948; *The Great South Land*, 1951; and in prose, *Conditional Culture*, 1938, and (with John Ingamells), *At a Boundary*, 1941.

'J.R.', *see* 'R., J.'

'KATE, RICKETTY' (Mrs A. J. Filson), 1898. Born at Wyalong, N.S.W., and educated at Cleveland Street High School, Sydney, and a Sydney business college. Engaged in secretarial work and was for nine years manager of *The Church Standard*. Mrs Filson has been for many years an invalid, and this and a strong sense of humour gave rise to her pen-name. Publications: *Rhymes and Whimsies*, 1937; *Out of the Dust*, 1939; and *Bralgah*, 1943.

BIOGRAPHIES

KEOGH, LESBIA, *see* HARFORD, LESBIA (VENNER).

LAVATER, LOUIS, 1867.
Born at St. Kilda, Vic., and educated at St. Kilda Grammar School and the University of Melbourne. Poet and composer of music; has been president or vice-president of various musical associations, has contributed musical criticisms to various Victorian newspapers, and has adjudicated in musical competitions at Eisteddfods in various Australian states. Publications include *This Green Mortality,* 1923. He also edited an anthology, *The Sonnet in Australasia,* 1926, and the magazine, *Verse.*

LEWIS, MURIEL ARMSTRONG.
Born in Brisbane and educated at the Brisbane Girls' Grammar School. She taught the pianoforte for some years in Q., and English on various N.S.W. stations and in France. She has so far published no book.

LITCHFIELD, JESSIE SINCLAIR, *née* Phillips.
One of the pioneers of the Northern Territory. Born at Ashfield, N.S.W., and educated at state schools. Went to Darwin, N.T., and there married. Spent many years on mining fields and coastal areas of the Territory, and for two years edited the *Northern Territory Times.* Conducted a small lending library in Sydney and now conducts it in Darwin. Is a member of the Darwin Chamber of Commerce, and stood for the Federal Parliament at the last elections.

MACARTNEY, FREDERICK THOMAS BENNETT, 1887.
Born and educated in Melbourne. Became clerk, freelance journalist, shorthand reporter, and bookkeeper on a Riverina sheep station, and was for some years Clerk of Courts, Public Trustee and Sheriff in the Northern Territory. Has delivered Commonwealth Literary Fund lectures at several Australian universities. Married. Publications: *Preferences* (a selection from several previous books of verse), 1941; *Ode of Our Times,* 1944; *Gaily the Troubadour,* 1946; and *Tripod for Homeward Incense,* 1947. Edited *Australian Poetry, 1947.*

McAULEY, JAMES (PHILLIP), M.A. (Syd.), 1917.
Born at Lakemba, N.S.W., and educated at Fort Street High School, Sydney, and the University of Sydney. Worked in the Australian Army Directorate of Research and Civil Affairs, 1943-4, and in the Australian Army School of Civil Affairs, 1945; now Senior Lecturer in Colonial Administration at the Australian School of Pacific Administration. Married. Publication: *Under Aldebaran,* 1946.

BIOGRAPHIES

McCRAE, HUGH (RAYMOND), 1876.
Born at Hawthorn, Vic.; son of George Gordon McCrae, well known poet and man of letters in the days of Gordon and Marcus Clarke. Was articled to an architect, but soon abandoned office work for humorous drawings and serious verse. Has acted in Australia and the United States, and for a while edited *The New Triad*. Now lives at Camden, N.S.W. Married. Publications include *Satyrs and Sunlight*, 1911; *Colombine*, 1920; *Idyllia*, 1924; *Satyrs and Sunlight* (including most of the poems in the previous books), 1928; *Poems* (this includes some, but by no means all, his previous published poems, and some new poems), 1939; *Forests of Pan*, 1944; *Voice of the Forest*, 1945; and *The Ship of Heaven* (a fairy opera), 1951; also, in prose, *Story-Book Only*, 1948 (this includes *The Du Poissey Anecdotes*); and *My Father and My Father's Friends*, 1935.

McCUAIG, RONALD, 1908.
Born at Newcastle, N.S.W., and educated at private schools in Sydney. At seventeen became a warehouseman and at twenty a radio journalist. In 1939 travelled round the world, and has since been a member of the staffs of *Smith's Weekly*, the *Sydney Morning Herald* and the *Bulletin*. Publications include *Quod Ronald McCuaig*, 1946, which collects poems from several booklets; and a small volume of stories and criticisms, *Tales Out of Bed*, 1944.

MACKELLAR, (ISOBEL MARION) DOROTHEA.
Born in Sydney and educated privately. Has travelled over much of Europe, especially Spain; and also in America, Morocco, Egypt, China and Japan. Lives in Sydney. Publications: *The Closed Door*, 1911; *The Witch-Maid*, 1914; *Dreamharbour*, 1923; and *Fancy Dress*, 1926; she has also written one novel and collaborated in two others.

McKELLAR, JOHN ALEXANDER ROSS, 1904-1932.
Born at Dulwich Hill, N.S.W., and educated at the Sydney High School. Was fond of sport, and also of music and the Latin and Greek classics. At fifteen, entered the service of the Bank of N.S.W., in which he showed exceptional ability. Publication: *Collected Poems*, 1946, which included the contents of a previous book of verse, *Twenty-Six*, 1931.

MACKENZIE, KENNETH (SEAFORTH), 1913.
Born in Perth, and educated at Perth Grammar School and at the University of Western Australia. After studying law and agriculture, settled in Sydney and became a journalist, but is

now an agricultural labourer. Married. Publications include *The Moonlit Doorway*, 1934; and three novels, *The Young Desire It*, 1937; *Chosen People*, 1938; and *Dead Men Rising*, 1951.

MANN, LEONARD, LL.M. (Melb.), 1895.

Born in Melbourne, and educated at a state school, Wesley College and the University of Melbourne. Served in the A.I.F. in the first World War. Married. Publications: *The Plumed Voice*, 1938; *Poems from the Mask*, 1941; *The Delectable Mountains*, 1944; also several novels, including *Flesh in Armour*, 1932, which was awarded the gold medal of the Australian Literature Society for the best Australian novel of the year; *A Murder in Sydney*, 1937; *Mountain Flat*, 1939; and *The Go-Getter*, 1942.

'MAURICE, FURNLEY', see WILMOT, FRANK (LESLIE THOMSON).

MAXWELL, IAN (RAMSAY), B.A., LL.B. (Melb.), B.Litt. (Oxon), 'R', 1901. Born at Upper Hawthorn, Vic. Educated at Scotch College, Melbourne, and the Universities of Melbourne and Oxford. Practised in Melbourne as a barrister, was lecturer in English at the Universities of Copenhagen and Sydney, and is now Professor of English in the University of Melbourne. Married. He has hitherto published no book of verse, but his other publications include *French Farce and John Heywood*, 1946.

MOLL, ERNEST GEORGE, M.A. (Harvard), 1900.

Born at Murtoa, Vic., and educated at N.S.W. state schools and the University of Harvard. Professor of English at the University of Oregon, but has retained his Australian citizenship and was in Australia 1939-40 as exchange lecturer in the N.S.W. Teachers' College. Married. Publications include, besides several American books of verse, the following, whose contents are Australian and which were published in Australia: *Cut from Mulga*, 1940; *Brief Waters*, 1945; *Beware the Cuckoo*, 1947; and *The Waterhole*, 1948.

MOORE, TOM INGLIS, B.A. (Syd.), M.A. (Oxon), 1901.

Born at Camden, N.S.W. Educated at Sydney Grammar School and the Universities of Sydney and Oxford, to the latter of which he won a travelling scholarship. Lectured in English in the United States, was Associate Professor of English in the University of the Philippines, and afterwards became a leader

BIOGRAPHIES

. writer on the *Sydney Morning Herald*. Married. Served in the war in the artillery and Army Education Service. Now senior lecturer in Pacific Studies, Canberra University College, and has lectured at several universities for the Commonwealth Literary Fund. Publications include *Adagio in Blue*, 1938; *Emu Parade*, 1941, and *We're Going Through* (radio verse play), 1945; edited *Australian Poetry, 1946,* and (with William Moore) *Best Australian One-Act Plays,* 1937. Has also published a book of criticism, *Six Australian Poets,* 1942, and a novel, *The Half-way Sun,* 1935.

MUDIE, IAN (MAYELSTON), 1911.
Born at Hawthorn, S.A. Educated at Scotch College, Adelaide, but says that carrying a swag constituted part of his education. A freelance journalist, with excursions into various other occupations. Married. Publications: *Poems 1934-44*, 1945, which collected most of the contents of several previous books of verse; also edited *Poets at War* (an anthology of poems by Australian servicemen), 1944.

NEILSON, (JOHN) SHAW, 1872-1942.
Born at Penola, S.A. Had little school education. At nine years of age his parents took him to Victoria, where he led the life of the ordinary bush worker, working on orchards and as a quarryman's labourer. During his last years he was appointed to a minor position in a Melbourne government department and awarded a small Commonwealth literary pension. Publications: *Collected Poems,* 1934, which included the contents of several previous booklets; *Beauty Imposes,* 1938; and *The Unpublished Poems of Shaw Neilson* (ed. by James Devaney), 1947.

O'LEARY, SHAWN (HAMILTON), B.A. (Q.), 1916.
Born at Ipswich, Q., and educated at various schools and the University of Queensland. Journalist, but has also given radio talks for the A.B.C. and B.B.C. Has lived in every Australian capital city, and now lives in London. Served with the A.I.F. in the Middle East and New Guinea and Borneo. Married. Publication: *Spikenard and Bayonet,* 1942.

PALMER, (EDWARD) VANCE, 1885.
Born at Bundaberg, Q. Educated at the Boys' Grammar School, Ipswich, Q. At twenty-one went to London, where he contributed short stories to various English magazines. In 1907 travelled in Russia, Siberia and the Far East. After two more

years, mainly on Australian stations, again became a freelance journalist in London. A member of the A.I.F. in the first World War. Lecturer and broadcaster as well as writer. Married to Nettie Palmer. Publications include *The Forerunners*, 1915; and *The Camp*, 1920; *The World of Men* (prose sketches), 1915; *The Black Horse and Other Plays*, 1924; and *Hail Tomorrow*, 1947; also a number of novels, including *The Passage*, 1930; *Men are Human*, 1930; and *Golconda*, 1948; two books of short stories, *Separate Lives*, 1931; and *Sea and Spinifex*, 1934; and several collections of biographical sketches.

'R', *see* MAXWELL, I. R.

'R., J.' This author wishes to remain anonymous.

'RICKETTY KATE', *see* 'KATE, RICKETTY'.

RIDDELL, ELIZABETH (Mrs E. N. Greatorex), 1909.
Born at Napier, N.Z. Educated at the Convent of the Sacred Heart, Timaru, N.Z. Was a journalist on the staff of several Sydney newspapers, representative in New York of the Sydney *Daily Mirror*, and later correspondent in Europe. Now editor of *Woman and Glamor*. Publications: *The Untrammelled*, 1940; *Poems*, 1948.

SHAW, WINIFRED (MAITLAND, Mrs R. M. Taplyn), 1905.
Born at Singleton, N.S.W., and educated at home. Lived at Singleton until her marriage, after which she left for Singapore and worked in a government office. During the war she was interned in Changi prison camp; she is now living in London. Publications: *The Aspen Tree and Other Verses*, 1920; *The Yellow Cloak and Other Poems*, 1922; *Babylon*, 1924.

SLESSOR, KENNETH, 1901.
Born at Orange, N.S.W., and educated at Mowbray House School, Chatswood, and the Church of England Grammar School, Sydney. Became a reporter on the Sydney *Sun*, joined the staff of Melbourne *Punch* and later of the Melbourne *Herald*, and was appointed editor-in-chief of Smith's Newspapers. Was Commonwealth representative with the A.I.F. and has now rejoined the staff of the Sydney *Sun*. Widower. Publications: *One Hundred Poems*, 1944, which collects poems from several previous books; also edited *Australian Poetry, 1945*.

STEWART, DOUGLAS (ALEXANDER), 1913.
Born at Eltham, N.Z. Educated at New Plymouth Boys' High School and Victoria University College, N.Z. After working on the staff of several New Zealand newspapers, migrated to

Australia and now edits the Red Page of the *Bulletin*. Married. Publications, besides several books of verse which were written while he lived in New Zealand: *Elegy for an Airman*, 1940; *Sonnets to the Unknown Soldier*, 1941; *The Dosser in Spring-time*, 1946; *Glencoe*, 1947; four plays, *Ned Kelly*, 1943; *The Fire on the Snow and The Golden Lover*, 1944; and *Ship-wreck*, 1947; and *The Flesh and the Spirit* (critical essays), 1948. Edited *Australian Poetry, 1941*.

STEWART, HAROLD (FREDERICK), 1916.
Born at Drummoyne, N.S.W. Educated at the Drummoyne Public School, Fort Street Boys' High School, the Sydney Conservatorium of Music and the University of Sydney. Poet and art critic; was during the war attached to the Directorate of Research and Civil Affairs. Publication: *Phoenix Wings*, 1948. His long poem, *Orpheus*, which has not yet been published, won a prize in the *Sydney Morning Herald* verse competition in 1949.

VREPONT, BRIAN (Benjamin Arthur Truebridge), 1882.
Born at North Carlton, Vic. Educated at a state school and privately. Became chief study teacher of the violin at the University Conservatorium, Melbourne, and also a medical masseur. Practised journalism and wandered about Australia on foot, horse and bicycle. Married. Publications: *The Miracle*, 1940 (which was awarded the C. J. Dennis Memorial Prize for the best poem of 1939); and *Beyond the Claw*, 1943.

WEBB, FRANCIS, 1925.
Born in Adelaide and educated at the Christian Brothers' High School, Lewisham, N.S.W. Engaged in clerical work, and then travelled to Canada, where he was for some time on the editorial staff of the Macmillan Co., Toronto. Now lives in Sydney. Publication: *A Drum for Ben Boyd*, 1948, which was awarded the Grace Leven Prize for the best book of verse of the year.

WILMOT, FRANK (LESLIE THOMSON), 'FURNLEY MAURICE', 1881-1942. Born at Richmond, Vic., son of a pioneer of the socialist movement in Australia. Became printer, publisher, bookseller and finally manager of the Melbourne University Press. Was one of the leaders of the principal Melbourne literary societies and a member of the Advisory Board of the Commonwealth Literary Fund, and lectured for that Fund at the University of Melbourne. A notable critic as well as poet. Married. Publications include *Poems*, 1944, a selection by

BIOGRAPHIES

Percival Serle which collected poems from a number of Wilmot's books, and *Romance* (essays), 1922. He compiled *Path to Parnassus* (a school anthology), 1940; assisted in the compilation of Serle's *Australasian Anthology*, 1927; and compiled, with G. H. Cowling, *Australian Essays*, 1935.

WRIGHT, JUDITH (ARUNDEL, Mrs J. P. McKinney), 1915. Born at Armidale, N.S.W., and educated at the New England Girls' School and the University of Sydney. Has been stenographer, private secretary and Statistical Research Officer to the University of Queensland. Publications: *The Moving Image*, 1946; and *Woman to Man*, 1949. Edited *Australian Poetry, 1948*.